JAMES JOYCE
in
PADUA

James Joyce, age about 30, in Trieste, circa 1912.

JAMES JOYCE
in
PADUA

Edited, translated
and introduced by
LOUIS BERRONE

Random House   New York

Library of Congress Cataloging in Publication Data
Joyce, James, 1882–1941.
James Joyce in Padua.
Bibliography: p.
I. Berrone, Louis. II. Title.
PR6019.09A23   823'.9'12   77–6027
ISBN 0–394–40990–6

DESIGN BY LILLY LANGOTSKY

Manufactured in the United States of America
2 4 6 8 9 7 5 3
First Edition

This book is for my wife
NINA
and children—
CARLA, TERRY, LISA, ANNIE, and JULIE,
as is the durée *and the* élan vital *in it.*

Epigraph

as a home cured emigrant in Paddyouare far
below on our sealevel
—James Joyce
Finnegans Wake, 463

In Padua, far beyond the sea
—Sir Walter Scott
The Lay of the Last Minstrel

Contents

———◆◉◆———

List of Illustrations

List of Illustrations

INTRODUCTION

Joyce wrote the two essays, "The Universal Literary Influence of the Renaissance" and "The Centenary of Charles Dickens," late in April 1912. They were parts of an examination that he sat for at the University of Padua in order to be certified as an English teacher in Italy. He was thirty years old, alert, and quite confident of his intellectual powers. When he was fifteen he had written the prizewinning composition in English at Belvedere College, Dublin: the best in his grade in Ireland. He won that prize again at Belvedere in the following year. The Padua exams provided him with another chance to test, in a phrase from his Dickens essay, the "ancient cunning" of his hand. Why should he not succeed in this competition as he had writing his schoolboy English essays in Ireland? He assuredly had strong incentives to excel. Many personal problems pressed down on him in Trieste, and he felt an urgent need to escape from teaching private English lessons there.

He did in fact surpass, by well over fifty points, all other students who took similar examinations at that time at the University of Padua. We might well expect this from a master prose stylist such as Joyce, but the essays also astonish us because they provide so many important insights into his critical thought and ideas implicit in his fiction. We may recall that in April 1912 he had already written three chapters of *A Portrait of the Artist as a Young Man* and had *Ulysses* in mind. Though the essays were impromptu answers to examination questions, we cannot imagine Joyce improving upon them very much.

The first essay, written in Italian, clearly expresses the point that one of the effects of the Renaissance on literature was to stress external, sensate experiences at the expense of the inner life. Joyce's high opinion of Dickens in his second essay comes as a pleasant surprise. Critics have commented on links between the authors, but no one has suspected that we should ever see Joyce praise "the great Cockney" in so many words and in such a well-balanced way. Here are some sixty-five-year-old ideas about modern life and literature that have a new, young sound. The essays are seminal. Readers will admire them for many reasons; one of the most important will be that they reveal Joyce's strength of mind in expressing spontaneous thoughts that were yet consonant with those of the carefully considered formal lectures he had given a month earlier.

At first glance it might seem that the two essays in this book are contradictory or at least in paradoxical opposition to each other; but we may see that Joyce was following, to some extent, a pattern that he set in his March 1912 Trieste lectures, "Realism and Idealism in English Literature (Daniel Defoe–William Blake)."[1] The two Paduan essays, the first on an idealistic theme and the second on a novelist who was grounded in reality, do, like the Defoe–Blake lectures, complement each other. Joyce's ability to express inner states of life in his fiction by means of selecting significant external events and realistic details may be envisioned by contemplating the critical essays together. Such a contemplation might well begin with the last paragraph of Yeats's "Discoveries" (1906), where he implies that unless a Shelley and a Dickens can be merged in one body man will remain forever fragmented.[2] Although Joyce does not mention Shelley in his idealistic Renaissance essay, he does delve into spiritual issues in it that might have pleased Yeats, from whom he seems to have derived some important material for both his Blake lecture and his Renaissance essay.

If there was one person in Ireland whose intellect, imagination, and art were as high-minded as his own, it was Yeats. And it was Yeats who had written so well on Blake that Joyce would naturally be inclined to draw on him for ideas for his own Blake lecture. Both Joyce and Yeats wanted to fuse spirit and matter; and if Joyce became more of a realist than Yeats, it may be as a result of reading Defoe and Dickens, as well as other more modern realists, such as Ibsen and Flaubert. Yet, along with the influence of Dujardin's *Les lauriers sont coupés* and other currents of inner-oriented art and thought that crossed Joyce's mind, Yeats's and his friend Arthur Symons's symbolist aesthetics were crucial in causing Joyce to write *A Portrait* as a stream-of-consciousness novel; and their aesthetics are reflected in Joyce's Paduan essay on the Renaissance. Also, Yeats helped Joyce before and during his exile. He introduced Joyce to Symons in 1902 and to Ezra Pound in 1913. If it were not for Yeats's friendly interest and introductions, Joyce might not have surmounted his many misfortunes in Europe, which included the unfortunate results of his writing the two Paduan essays.

Joyce and his family lived through many years of hardship in Trieste, and 1912, when Joyce journeyed by train to Padua to write the exams, was no exception. He was earning his living by giving private English lessons in his third-floor apartment at Via Barriera Vecchia 32 and in his students' homes. His income barely provided for a household that included his wife Nora, his two children, Giorgio and Lucia, and his sister Eileen.

He had published a book of poems, *Chamber Music,* in 1907, but received no royalties from it. Two different publishers had contracted with him to bring out his collection of short stories, *Dubliners,* and both had reneged. Prior to 1912 he had taught for the Berlitz School in Pola and Trieste, had written some articles for the Triestine newspaper, *Il Piccolo della Sera,* and had ventured unsuccessfully into various business enterprises. He had opened a movie house, the Volta Theatre, in 1909 in Ireland, which subsequently failed. He had started to import Irish tweeds to Trieste, but that venture also proved unprofitable. He had considered exporting skyrockets to Ireland, but then thought that this was too dangerous. Although his brother Stanislaus had also lived in Trieste since 1905 and had saved the Joyces from starvation and eviction on numerous occasions and acted as his brother's literary whetstone, he could not resolve every problem; they often quarreled and for short periods were cold and at a distance from each other.

Joyce suffered severely from rheumatism and iritis. He went on heavy drinking sprees and through serious stages of depression. His "publisher" George Roberts wrote to him in February 1911 that all references to King Edward VII must be cut from "Ivy Day in the Committee Room," a story in *Dubliners.* Joyce was very much disturbed; he argued with Nora, and then threw the first three chapters of *A Portrait* into the fire. Eileen, entering the room and seeing what he had done, quickly rescued the manuscript, burning her fingers doing so. On the following morning Joyce, in gratitude, bought Eileen three bars of varicolored soap and a pair of mittens and told her that there were parts of the novel he could never have rewritten from memory.[3] He had a mental block that prevented him from finishing *A Portrait* until *Dubliners* was published.

Still fighting for the publication of his short stories, he wrote directly to King George V on August 1, 1911 to try to get a ruling on references to the king's father, Edward VII, in *Dubliners*. On August 11 Joyce received a letter from the king's secretary in which he stated that the king could not "express his opinion in such cases."[4] Joyce's mixed feelings upon receiving a reply from Buckingham Palace addressed to him at Via Barriera Vecchia 32 are quite humanly and humorously dramatized by Stelio Crise in *Epiphanies and Phadographs: Joyce e Trieste*. Crise imagines Joyce reading the letter, then walking across the street to the Caffè Bizantino, having a quiet morning drink, and thinking that he is in correspondence with the king of England and is throwing away his life at ten crowns an hour on private English lessons.[5] The royal response spurred Joyce to write an open letter attacking censorship in England and Ireland, which was partially printed in *The Northern Whig* in Belfast on August 26 and fully printed in *Sinn Fein* in Dublin on September 1. But even this letter did not persuade Roberts to publish *Dubliners*. The episode may have been a moral victory for Joyce, but that was all.

Trieste, however, was not without its high moments. We should not forget Joyce's happiness at the birth of his children, his love for Nora and his appreciation of his friends; his sense of accomplishment in completing *Chamber Music, Dubliners, A Portrait*; his excitement at beginning *Ulysses*. But, too, we should remember Kev cry in *Finnegans Wake*, "And trieste, ah trieste ate I my liver!"[6] And we can understand Joyce's desire for a secure teaching post and his hope that he could find it in Italy.

In the fall of 1911 Joyce wrote to several Italian educational officials enquiring about work as a teacher and trying to find out what he had to do to qualify for such a position. In the meantime he gave two lectures on Defoe and Blake at the Università Popolare Triestina in March 1912; this was his second lecture series there. In April and May of 1907 he had given three lectures on Irish subjects at the Università: "Ireland, Island of Saints and Sages," "James Clarence Mangan," and "The Irish Literary Renaissance." His decision to discuss English literature for his 1912 lectures may have been prompted by the prospect of teaching English in Italy and the intimation that he would probably be examined in that field beforehand.

Joyce passed with distinction the exams that he took at the University of Padua in 1912. Richard Ellmann tells how he traveled from Trieste to Padua and took the series of examinations in English and Italian from April 24 to April 26.[7] On the 25th Joyce wrote the following postcard to his brother Stanislaus:

> Padua is full up of the overflowings of Venice. When I arrived I had to make a pilgrimage from door to door before I got a room. Consequently things are dearer. Today, I had to write my English theme—*Dickens* and saw my English examiner, an old, ugly spinster from the tight little island—a most dreadful *fRump* (reformed spelling). The orals and the trial lesson will not be fixed for some days. I cannot remain on another 5 or 6 days so that I shall probably return tomorrow and wait a telegram to come again for 1 day. That will cost 25 crowns but to remain on would cost more besides the disorder of the lessons in Trieste.[8]

Ellmann records the excellent grades Joyce received—421 out of a possible 450 points—and explains that the refusal of Italian authorities to recognize his Dublin degree prevented him from receiving a teaching diploma in spite of his good score.

Some documents in the James Joyce Collection at Cornell University and some of Joyce's letters of that period help to record more fully the story of his examinations at Padua. One of the earliest is a letter to Joyce (November 15, 1911) from the Secretary of the Faculty of Philosophy and Letters at the

Introduction

University of Padua.[9] The Secretary explains that the Royal Decree of 1908, governing the examinations for a teacher's diploma, distinguishes between primary and secondary certification. He indicates that because Joyce is a college graduate he might aspire to the secondary school diploma. He adds that the Higher Council of Education must approve his academic credentials, and he suggests that Joyce ask immediately for this approval so that he can take the examinations during the next session at the University, probably in April 1912.

In a postcard to Joyce dated November 20, 1911, C. Meroggi, the principal of the Istituto Tecnico at Como, informs Joyce that although the opening for an English teacher in his school has not been filled, the competitive exams have been in session since October 15 and that, in any case, he would need a teacher's diploma in order to be accepted as an entrant in the hiring competition.[10] He tells Joyce that he must enroll in an Italian university session of examinations for a teacher's diploma if he wishes to qualify for a future position.

The Secretary of the Higher Council of the Ministry of Education in Rome, Signor Ebiani, in a letter to Joyce dated November 29, 1911, informs him that an authenticated copy of his college diploma would suffice for the purpose Joyce had stated in a postcard to Ebiani's office[11]—we may infer that the "purpose" was to earn the diploma that would permit him to teach English. In another letter to Joyce, dated November 30, 1911, Ebiani informs him that he has received the documents Joyce has sent on to him and that he has forwarded them to the Minister of Education, since the Higher Council could not consider anything that did not come to them direct from the Ministry.[12] That the documents were in order, except for establishing the equipollence of the degrees, is evinced by the ministerial disposition from Rome on April 19, 1912, to Rector Rossi at the University authorizing him to admit Joyce to the examinations, which were to be held on April 24, 25, and 26. The approximately four-and-a-half-month lapse of time between Ebiani's second letter and the decision to accept Joyce for the exams does seem to be inordinate. The Rector notified Joyce on April 20 that he was conditionally accepted as a candidate for the examinations, and Joyce answered on April 21 that he would take them. By this time they were only three days away. Unless there were intervening letters or circumstances that we do not know about, it would seem that not only did Joyce write his essays in a test situation (against the clock and under his examiner's watchful eye) but also that they were, in the strictest sense, impromptu. For each exam he was given a choice of two subjects.

The earliest document in Joyce's file at Padua is a telegram dated April 19 from the Minister of Education in Rome to Vittorio Rossi, Rector of the University of Padua. It reads in translation:

The Ministry authorizes Your Excellency to admit to the next scheduled examinations at this university for the teacher's diploma of the English language for secondary schools Mr. James Joyce British subject with a diploma in neo-Latin from the University of Ireland presently living in Trieste via della barriera vecchia 32 third floor. In giving this communication to the interested party and in informing him to be present on the prescribed days to take the examinations, advise him that his acceptance as well as the efficacy and validity of the exams themselves on each effect of the law are subordinate to the judgment that the Higher Council will be called on to pronounce on the equipollence of his university under-graduate qualifications. Before the judgment of the Council is given no diploma or certificate relative to the examination can be awarded to Mr. Joyce.

Vittorio Rossi telegraphed Joyce the following day:

Per ministerial disposition you are admitted to the examination for the secondary school teacher's diploma of English. The worth of the examination however subordinated to the judgment that the Higher Council will give on the equipollence of your university undergraduate qualifications—examinations written fixed days 24, 25, 26 consecutively; you should, therefore, be here on the day of the 24th at 8 o'clock.

Joyce responded the next day with a short letter in Italian, saying that he would be present on Wednesday, April 24 at eight A.M.

Eugenio Borsatti, a Triestine bookseller and editor who worked in F. K. Schimpf's bookstore when Joyce traded there, recalled that Joyce was furious with the English spinster who administered the tests.[13] Joyce must have been under considerable pressure as an Irish exile living in an Austrian city and taking his exams in an Italian university under the thumb of a disagreeable English schoolmistress. As well as supervising the essays of the first two days, she administered the third section of the examination on April 26: dictation from Sir Edward Bulwer-Lytton's *The Last Days of Pompeii*. The fourth section, a translation into English of a segment from *Ricordi di mia vita* by Pietro Colletta, the Neapolitan general and historian, followed later on the same day. The English examiner, Margherita de Rénoche, was also a member of the examination commission. Her signature appears at the end of the Official Record, together with those of the other members.

Joyce took the orals and presented his trial lesson on April 30. The requirements for the orals and the points he received for them are given in the Official Record, as are also the grades he received for his lesson plans on (1) "The Good Parson of Chaucer" and (2) "The Rise of the Drama." A scrap of paper in Joyce's Padua file, probably written by the examiner, contains two sets of instructions: (1) "Paraphrase into modern

English and translate into Italian the lines [The Good Parson] 'A good man was there of religioun . . . wolde he teche,' " and (2) "Give a short account of the rise of the Drama in England." Since no written records of the test plan are included in Joyce's file, we may assume that it also was presented orally to simulate a classroom situation, and that his examiner simply wrote down the points she allotted him for each part, which were then filled in on his Official Record.

Joyce's intellectual acumen is evident in the essays and reflected in his grades. He responded intelligently to the oral questions in English and to other questions on English literature put to him in Italian (for which he received 95 out of a possible 100 points). He also presented a lesson plan (for which he earned 50 out of 50 possible points). The sad note is that, despite his brilliant success in these examinations, the diploma was irrevocably denied him.

The news that his application for the diploma had been turned down was officially broken to Joyce by Rector Rossi in a letter addressed to him in Trieste on August 1, 1912. For the most part the letter consisted of a quotation from the Ministry of Education (dated June 25, 1912).[14] The letter from the Ministry indicated that its Higher Council, meeting on June 14, 1912, did not recognize the equipollence of Joyce's 1902 degree from the University of Dublin with that of an Italian university. The Ministry, acting in accordance with the telegram of April 19, 1912, to the Rector (which stated that the condition under which Joyce would be accepted for the examinations was that equipollence be established), annulled the validity of the examinations. Joyce had returned to Ireland by the time this letter arrived in Trieste, and its contents were probably first broached to him in a letter from Stanislaus early in August.[15]

Joyce, in a postcard from Galway dated August 10, gives his brother a Roland for his Oliver, a *quid pro quo* to make them even in their exchange of depressing news. Joyce informs Stanislaus that Roberts, who had signed a contract to publish *Dubliners*, had reneged on it and had suggested that he turn over the already printed sheets to the editor who had first rejected the book, Grant Richards.[16] Joyce's consternation over *Dubliners*, mingled with his confusion and perplexity about Padua and his examination results, left him with the feeling that he was being pursued by a jinx, a *scalogna*. He rallies somewhat at the close of the card to say that he will write to the Board of Education in London to find out why the British degree was not considered valid for *"examination* purposes in Italy," and in another postcard to Stanislaus postmarked August 14 he states that he has done so.[17] A reply from the Board of Education, Whitehall, London, on August 15 informs Joyce that there was no agreement between the British and Italian offices of education on reciprocal acknowledgments of university degrees.[18] According to the Board, the Italian government was free to recognize British degrees on whatever conditions they chose to establish. On August 18 Joyce told Stanislaus that the Board of Education could do nothing to help him,[19] and on August 19 he informed Nora that he had received an answer from London demonstrating his usual luck![20]

Yet Joyce with his usual pertinacity did not easily concede the point to the Ministry of Education. He appealed to Senator Guido Mazzoni, a poet and lecturer whom he had met in Trieste, for help. In a letter dated January 1913, Joyce asked Stanislaus for a copy of Arthur Symons's review of *Chamber Music* to send to Senator Mazzoni, who had agreed to try to help him resolve the Padua case.[21] He also appealed to the Consul, Carlo Galli, but neither Mazzoni nor Galli were able to help him.[22] The formidable intellectual exertions Joyce put into the Paduan essays and the hydra-headed hardships he and his family suffered failed to bring about any gainful results.

The Renaissance essay is an important discovery. Other than the statement in the official Report of the University of Padua, translated by Ellmann in *James Joyce*, that Joyce wrote a composition in Italian for which he received 30 out of 50 possible points (and Pinguentini's reference to it in *Joyce in Italia*), we have until now had no knowledge of its present existence or contents.

Though Joyce did not benefit directly from writing the essays in 1912, we may from reading them today. He made few comments about Charles Dickens in his letters, criticism, or in his recorded conversations.[23] Weldon Thornton, Don Gifford and Robert J. Seidman have pointed out allusions to Dickens in *Ulysses;* Adaline Glasheen and James S. Atherton have done so in their writings on *Finnegans Wake*. Other critics have also noted allusions to Dickens or affinities with him in Joyce's works. Stanislaus Joyce says in *My Brother's Keeper* that from what he recalls of his brother's reading interests when the family lived on Millbourne Lane, Drumcondra, and Joyce was twelve and when they lived on North Richmond Street and Joyce was in his early teens, he did not like Dickens.[24] After reading "The Centenary of Charles Dickens," we may see that by the time Joyce was thirty he did like many aspects of Dickens's work and had some worthwhile insights into it. His *Finnegans Wake* notebooks, moreover, contain specific references to Dickens and his works.

The library that Joyce left with his brother in Trieste (now in the possession of Nelly Joyce, Stanislaus's wife) includes five novels by Dickens. Richard Ellmann catalogues the library in his Appendix to *The Consciousness of James Joyce* (1977), and lists *Barnaby Rudge*, *Bleak House*, *David Copperfield*, *Nicholas Nickleby* (2 vols.), and *Oliver Twist* as being in the collection. Ellmann gives the publication date for all of these novels—with the exception of *Bleak House*—as 1812. Nelly Joyce kindly let me peruse the four volumes published in 1912 when I visited her in 1974. I noticed that they were obviously "read" books. Some words in *David Copperfield* had been underlined; some had been marked by X's. Three volumes, *David Copperfield*, *Oliver Twist*, and *Barnaby Rudge* belonged to the Centenary Edition published by Thomas Nelson and Sons, which may suggest that Joyce had at some time owned the complete edition, or at least a large selection from it.

The original texts of the facsimiles, printed here for the first time, remain in the Archivio Antico at the University of Padua. The transcriptions follow the manuscripts as closely as possible. I do not put accent marks on the Italian text where Joyce left them out, nor do I correct his other errors. In following Joseph Prescott's practice in his edition and translation of Joyce's lecture "Daniel Defoe," I spare the reader "a clutter of *sic*'s by reproducing Joyce's practice exactly and without comment."[25] My comments on the thesis-reader's markings appear after the facsimiles, transcriptions, translation, and Afterwords. I quote the passage and reproduce the marks for each correction before making observations on it. Under "Distinctive or Obscure Words and Phrases in Joyce's Paduan Essays" I try to clarify passages or to relate them to Joyce's other works.

I should like to express deep feelings of thanks to Professoressa Lucia Rossetti at the University of Padua for her assistance in finding the manuscripts and reproducing them; to Maurice Beebe at Temple University for his editorial help and criticism; to Michael Campo at Trinity College, Hartford, and Thomas Matrullo of Yale University for help with the translation and work with the Italian texts; to Bernard Benstock at the University of Illinois for reading my first writings on Joyce and Dickens and encouraging me to continue, which helped to motivate me to go to Padua; to Norman Silverstein, late of Queens College, who consistently helped me with this project; to Father James Coughlin, S.J., Dean of Fairfield University, and

Introduction

Nicholas Rinaldi, Chairman of the English Department at Fairfield, and my colleagues and the staff there for day-to-day help; to Fairfield University for granting me sabbatical leave to travel and write; to James Wilcox and Jean McNutt of Random House and to Adaline Glasheen for help in refining parts of this book; and to Jason Epstein of Random House, whose conversations and suggestions were fundamental to the work.

Notes to Introduction

---◆◉◆---

[1] See "William Blake" in *The Critical Writings of James Joyce*, ed. by Ellsworth Mason and Richard Ellmann (New York: Viking Press, 1959), and "Daniel Defoe," ed. by Joseph Prescott, *Buffalo Studies*, pub. by SUNY at Buffalo, Vol. I, No. 1, 1964.

[2] W. B. Yeats, "Discoveries," in *The Cutting of an Agate* in *W. B. Yeats: Essays and Introductions* (New York: Macmillan, 1968), p. 296. Ellmann in *The Identity of Yeats* (New York: Oxford University Press, 1964) seems to draw parallels between Yeats's advice to Joyce (1902) to fuse intellectual and folk material in his writing with Yeats's comments on fusing a Shelley and a Dickens in one body (a possibility Yeats also discussed in the Preface to *The Unicorn from the Stars*, 1908). See Ellmann, Chap. V, "The Pursuit of Spontaneity," pp. 86–91. Also see George Bornstein, *Yeats and Shelley* (Chicago and London: University of Chicago Press, 1970) for insights into Yeats's fusing Shelleyan and Dickensian qualities in his plays.

[3] See Richard Ellmann, *James Joyce* (New York: Oxford University Press, 1965), p. 325. Ellmann bases his account of this fire on an "Interview with Mrs. Eileen Joyce Schaurek, 1953; B.B.C. program, 'Portrait of James Joyce.' " Ftn., p. 784. Joyce in a letter to Miss Weaver, Jan. 6, 1920, gives a different account of it. See *Letters*, ed. by Stuart Gilbert (New York: Viking Press, 1957), Vol. I, p. 136. Also in *Selected Letters*, ed. by Ellmann (New York: The Viking Press, 1975), p. 247.

[4] MS. Cornell, No. 515, in Robert Scholes, *The Cornell Joyce Collection* (Cornell University Press, 1961), p. 87.

[5] Stelio Crise, *Epiphanies and Phadographs: Joyce e Trieste* (Milano: All'Insegna del Pesce D'oro, 1967), pp. 131–132.

[6] James Joyce, *Finnegans Wake* (New York: Viking Press, 1939), p. 301.

[7] Richard Ellmann, *James Joyce* (New York: Oxford University Press, 1965), pp. 331–332.

Notes to Introduction

[8] *Letters of James Joyce,* ed. by Richard Ellmann (Viking Press, 1966), Vol. II, pp. 294–295.

[9] MS. Cornell, No. 1289, in Scholes, p. 192.

[10] MS. Cornell, No. 882, in Scholes, p. 135.

[11] MS. Cornell, No. 884, in Scholes, p. 136.

[12] MS. Cornell, No. 885, in Scholes, p. 136.

[13] See Gianni Pinguentini, *James Joyce in Italia* (Verona: Linotipia Veronese del Ghidini e Fiorini, 1963), p. 197.

[14] MS. Cornell, No. 1290, in Scholes, p. 192.

[15] See *Letters,* Vol. II, p. 301, ftn. 1.

[16] *Letters,* Vol. II, p. 301.

[17] *Idem.*

[18] MS. Cornell, No. 433, in Scholes, p. 74.

[19] *Letters,* Vol. II, pp. 303–304.

[20] *Letters,* Vol. II, p. 304.

[21] *Letters,* Vol. II, pp. 322–323.

[22] See Ellmann, *James Joyce,* p. 332, and Pinguentini, p. 198.

[23] Joyce refers in passing to Dickensian characterization in "Drama and Life" (1900) and in his book review "Borlase and Son" (1903), *Critical Writings,* p. 40 and p. 140 respectively. Carola Giedion-Welcker remembers Joyce telling a man in Zurich who was reading Dickens that he should read Sterne instead. See "An Interview with Carola Giedion-Welcker and Maria Jolas," ed. by Richard M. Kain, *James Joyce Quarterly,* Vol. II, No. 2, Winter, 1974, p. 97.

[24] See Stanislaus Joyce, *My Brother's Keeper* (New York: The Viking Press, 1958), p. 61 and p. 79.

[25] Joseph Prescott, Editorial Note, "Daniel Defoe," *op. cit.,* p. 2.

JAMES JOYCE
in
PADUA

Joyce's Letter to the Rector of the University of Padua

VIA DELIA BARRIERA VECCHIA 32, III.
TRIESTE

(Austria)

Dr Alberini

Al Chiarissimo Signor Rettore
R. Università di Padova
Italia

Chiarissimo Signore

Ho ricevuto il dispaccio ch'Ella
ebbe la cortesia d'inviarmi e, secondo le istruzioni
ivi contenute, mi presenterò all'università per
l'esame d'abilitazione all'insegnamento della
lingua inglese mercoledì ventitré alle 8 ant.

Con doverosi ossequi

James Joyce B.A.

li 21 aprile 1912

VIA DELLA BARRIERA VECCHIA 32, III.

TRIESTE

(Austria)

Al Chiarissimo Signor Rettore
R. Università di Padova
Italia

Chiarissimo Signore

Ho ricevuto il dispaccio ch'Ella ebbe la cortesia d'inviarmi
e, secondo le istruzioni ivi contenute, mi presenterò all'università
per l'esame d'abilitazione all'insegnamento della lingua inglese
mercoledi venturo alle 8 ant.

Con doverosi ossequi

James Joyce B.A.

li 21 Aprile 1912

Joyce's Letter to the Rector of the University of Padua

VIA DELLA BARRIERA VECCHIA 32, III.

TRIESTE

(Austria)

To the Right Honorable Rector
R. University of Padua
Italy

Most Honored Sir

I received the telegram which you courteously sent me and, according to the instructions contained therein, I shall be at the university to take the examination for the teacher's diploma of the English language on this coming Wednesday at 8:00 A.M.

With dutiful respects,

James Joyce B.A.

The 21st of April 1912

R. UNIVERSITÀ DEGLI STUDI DI PADOVA

L'influenza letteraria universale del rinascimento

La dottrina evoluzionista, nella luce della quale la nostra società si bea, c'insegna che quando eravamo piccoli non eravamo ancora grandi; quindi, se poniamo il rinascimento europeo quale punto di divisione, dobbiamo arrivare a questa conclusione, che l'umanità fino a quell'epoca, non possedeva che l'anima ed il corpo di un fanciullo e, soltanto dopo quell'epoca, si sviluppò fisicamente e moralmente a tal segno da meritare il nome di adulto. È una conclusione molto drastica e poco convincente. Anzi (se non avessi paura di sembrare *laudator temporis acti*) vorrei combatterla a spada tratta. Il progresso tanto strombazzato di questo secolo consiste in gran parte in un proviglio di macchine il cui scopo è appunto quello di raccogliere in fretta e furia gli elementi sparpagliati dell'utile e dello scibile e di ridistribuirli ad ogni membro della collettività che sia in grado di pagare una tenue tassa. Convengo che questo sistema sociale possa vantarsi di grandi conquiste meccaniche, di grandi e benefiche scoperte. Basta, per convincersene, fare un elenco sommario di quelle che si vede nella strada di una grande città moderna: il tram elettrico, i fili telegrafici, l'umile e necessario postino, gli strilloni, le grandi aziende commerciali ecc. Ma in mezzo a questa civiltà complessa e multilaterale la mente umana terrorizzata quasi dalla grandezza materiale si perde, rinnega sé stessa e s'infrollisce. O dunque bisogna arrivare a questa conclusione che il materialismo odierno, che discende in linea retta dal rinascimento, atrofizza le facoltà spirituali dell'uomo, ne impedisce lo sviluppo, ne sminuzza la finezza? Vediamo.

All'epoca del rinascimento lo spirito umano lottava contro l'assolutismo scolastico contro quell'immenso (ed in molti riguardi mirabile) sistema filosofico che ha le sue ime fondamenta nel pensiero aristotelico, freddo, chiaro ed imperterrito, mentre la sua cima sorge alla luce vaga e misteriosa dell'ideologia cristiana. Ma se lo spirito umano lottava contro questo sistema non era perché il sistema in se stesso gli era alieno. Il giogo era dolce e lieve: ma era un giogo. E così quando i grandi ribelli del rinascimento proclamarono la buona novella alle genti europee che la tirannide non c'era più, che la tristezza e la sofferenza umana s'erano dileguate come nebbia al sorgere del sole, che l'uomo non era più un prigioniero, lo spirito umano sentì forse il fascino dell'ignoto, udì la voce del mondo visuale, tangibile, incostante, ove si vive e si muore, si pecca e si pente, ed, abbandonando la pace claustrale nella quale languiva, abbracciò il nuovo vangelo. Abbandonò la sua pace, la sua vera dimora, perché n'era stanco, come Dio stanco (mi si passi la parola alquanto irriverente) delle sue perfezioni divine chiama il creato fuori del

nulla, come la donna stanca della pace e delle quiete
che struggono il suo cuore volge lo sguardo verso
la vita tentatrice. Giordano Bruno stesso dice che
ogni potere, sia nella natura che nello spirito,
deve creare un potere opposto, senza il quale
non può realizzarsi ed aggiunge che in ogni
tale separazione c'è una tendenza alla riunione.
Il dualismo del sommo nolano rispecchia
fedelmente il fenomeno del rinascimento. E se
sembra un poco arbitrario il citare un
testimonio contro sè stesso, citare le stesse
parole di un novatore per condannare (o
almeno per giudicare) l'opera di cui fu l'
artefice rispondo che non faccio altro che seguire
l'esempio del Bruno stesso, il quale nella sua
lunga e persistente e cavillosa autodifesa
rivolge le armi dell'accusa contro l'accusatore.

Sarebbe facile riempire queste pagine
coi nomi dei grandi scrittori che l'ondata del
rinascimento portò alle nuvole (o più di lì),
lodare la grandezza delle loro opere, che, del
resto, nessuno pone in dubbio, e terminare
con la preghiera rituale: e sarebbe forse una
viltà poiché il recitare una litania non è
un'indagine filosofica. Il perno del problema
è altrove. Bisogna vedere che cosa veramente
significhi il rinascimento in quanto riguarda
la letteratura e verso quale fine, lieta o tragica,
ci conduca. Il rinascimento, per dirla in
poche parole, ha messo il giornalista nella
cattedra del monaco: vale a dire, ha deposto
una mentalità acuta, limitata e formale
per dare lo scettro ad una mentalità
facile ed estesa (come si suol dire nei

'63

giornali teatrali), una mentalità irrequieta ed
alquanto amorfa. Shakespeare e Lope de Vega
sono responsabili, fino ad un certo punto, per
il cinematografo. L'instancabile forza creatrice,
la calda e viva passionalità, il desiderio intenso
di vedere e di sentire, la curiosità sregolata
e diffusa degenerano dopo tre secoli in un
sensazionalismo frettoloso. Si potrebbe dire
infatti dell'uomo moderno che ha un'
epidermide invece di un'anima. Il potere
sensorio del suo organismo si è enormemente
sviluppato ma si è sviluppato a pregiudizio
nella facoltà spirituale. Il senso morale
e forse anche la forza d'immaginazione ci
mancano. Le opere letterarie più caratteristiche
che possediamo sono semplicemente amorali:
La Crisi di Marco Praga, Pelléas et Mélisande
di Maeterlinck, Crainquebille d'Anatole France,
Fumée di Turgenev. Forse le avrò prese piuttosto
a vanvera. Non monta: bastano per documentare
la tesi che sostengo. Un grande artista moderno
volendo musicare il sentimento dell'amore
riproduce, per quanto la sua arte glielo permette,
ogni pulsazione, ogni tremito, il più lieve
brivido, il più lieve sospiro; gli accordi s'
intrecciano e si fanno guerra sorda: si ama
mentre s'incrudelisce, si soffre quando e
quanto si gode, l'ira ed il dubbio lampeggiano
negli occhi degli amanti i cui corpi sono
una carne sola. Mettete Tristano ed Isotta
accanto all'Inferno e v'accorgerete come
l'odio del poeta segue la sua strada d'
abisso in abisso nella scia di un'idea che
s'intensifica e più intensamente il poeta

4)

R. UNIVERSITÀ DEGLI STUDI DI PADOVA

si consuma nel fuoco dell'idea dell'odio più truce diventa l'arte colla quale l'artista ci comunica la sua passione. L'una è un' arte di circostanze, l'altra è ideativa. Il compilatore d'attanti nel alto medioevo non si scomponeva quando si trovava in imbarazzo. Scriveva sulla tratta dubbiosa le parole: Hic sunt leones. Gli bastava l'idea della solitudine, il terrore delle strane bestie, l'ignoto. La nostra coltura ha tutt'un altro scopo: siamo avidi di dettagli. Il nostro genio letterario, per questo motivo, non parla che di colore locale, dell' ambiente, dell'atavismo: onde la ricerca febbrile del nuovo e dello strano, l'accumulazione di dettagli osservati o letti, l'ostentazione della coltura generale.

Il rinascimento a rigor di termini dovrebbe significare una nascita dopo una morte, una fecondità improvisa come quella di Sara dopo un lungo periodo di sterilità. Difatti, il rinascimento venne quando l'arte periva di perfezione formale ed il pensiero si perdeva in sottigliezze oziose. Un poema s'era ridotto un problema algebraico, posto e risolto secondo i regolamenti in simboli umani. Un filosofo era un sofista erudito come il Bellarmino e come Giovanni Mariana che, pur predicando al volgo la parola di Gesù, s'arrabbattava a costruire la difesa morale del tirannicidio.

5)

In mezzo a quest'afa il rinascimento entra come un uragano; ed in tutta Europa sorge un tumulto di voci e quantunque i cantori non ci siano più le loro opere sono come le conchiglie marine nelle quali, se porgiamo l'orecchio, udiamo riverberare la voce del mare.

Pare, a sentirla, un pianto: o almeno il nostro spirito l'interpreta così. Strana cosa davvero! Tutta la conquista moderna, dell'aria, della terra, del mare, della malattia, dell'ignoranza, si fonde, per così dire, nel crogiolo della mente e si trasforma in una piccola goccia d'acqua, in una lagrima. Se il rinascimento non avesse fatto altro, avrebbe fatto molto creando in noi stessi e nella nostra arte il senso della pietà per ogni essere che vive e spera e muore e s'illude. In questo almeno superiamo gli antichi: in questo il giornalista volgare è più grande del teologo.

James Joyce

"L'INFLUENZA LETTERARIA UNIVERSALE DEL RINASCIMENTO"

La dottrina evoluzionista, nella luce della quale la nostra società si bea, c'insegna che quando eravamo piccoli non eravamo ancora grandi: quindi, se poniamo il rinascimento européo quale punto di divisione, dobbiamo arrivare a questa conclusione, che l'umanità fino a quell'epoca, non possedeva che l'anima ed il corpo di un fanciullo e, soltanto dopo quell'epoca, si sviluppò fisicamente e moralmente a tal segno da meritare il nome di adulto. E una conclusione molto drastica e poco convincente. Anzi (se non avessi paura di sembrare *laudator temporis acti*) vorrei combatterla a spada tratta. Il progresso tanto strombazzato di questo secolo consiste in gran parte in un groviglio di macchine il cui scopo è appunto quello di raccogliere in fretta e furia gli elementi sparpagliati dell'utile e dello scibile e di ridistribuirli ad ogni membro della collettività che sia in grado di pagare una tenue tassa. Convengo che questo sistema sociale possa vantarsi di grandi conquiste meccaniche, de grandi e benefiche scoperte. Basta, per convincersene, fare un elenco sommario di quello che si vede nella strada di una grande città moderna: il tram elettrico, i fili telegrafici, l'umile e necessario postino, gli strilloni, le grandi aziende commerciali ecc. Ma in mezzo a questa civiltà complessa e multilaterale la mente umana terrorizzata quasi dalla grandezza materiale si perde; rinnega sè stessa e s'infrollisce. O dunque bisogna arrivare a questa conclusione che il materialismo odierno,—che discende in linea retta dal rinascimento,—atrofizza le facoltà spirituali dell'uomo, ne impedisce lo sviluppo, ne smussa la finezza? Vediamo.

All' epoca del rinascimento lo spirito umano lottava contro l'assolutismo scolastico contro quell'immenso (ed in molti riguardi mirabile) sistema filosofico che ha le sue ime fondamenta nel pensiero aristotelico, freddo, chiaro ed imperterrito, mentre la sua cima sorge alla luce vaga e misteriosa dell' ideologia cristiana. Ma se lo spirito umano lottava contro questo sistema non era perche il sistema in se stesso gli era alieno. Il giogo era dolce e lieve: ma era un giogo. E cosi quando i grandi ribelli del rinascimento proclamarono la buona novella alle genti europée che la tirannide non c'era più, che la tristezza e la sofferenza umane s'erano dileguate come nebbia al sorgere del sole, che l'uomo non era più un prigioniero, lo spirito umano sentì forse il fascino dell' ignoto, udì la voce del mondo visuale, tangibile, incostante, ove si vive e si muore, si pecca e si pente, ed, abbandonando la pace claustrale nella quale languiva, abbracciò il nuovo vangelo. Abbandonò la sua pace, la sua vera dimora, perchè n'era stanco, come Dio stanco (mi si passi la parola alquanto irriverente) delle sue perfezioni divine chiama il creato fuori del nulla, come la donna stanca della pace e della quiete che struggono il suo cuore volge lo sguardo verso la vita tentatrice. Giordano Bruno stesso dice che ogni potere, sia nella natura che nello spirito, deve creare un potere opposto, senza il quale non può realizzarsi ed aggiunge che in ogni tale separazione c'è una tendenza alla riunione. Il dualismo del sommo nolano rispecchia fedelmente il fenomeno del rinascimento. E se sembra un poco arbitrario il citare un testimonio contro sè stesso, citare le stesse parole di un novatore per condannare (o almeno per giudicare) l'opera di cui fu l'artefice rispondo che non faccio altro che seguire l'esempio del Bruno stesso, il quale nella sua lunga e persistente e cavillosa autodifesa rivolge le armi dell'accusa contro l'accusatore.

Sarebbe facile riempire queste pagine coi nomi dei grandi scrittori che l'ondata del rinascimento portò alle nuvole (o giù di lì), lodare la grandezza delle loro opere, che, del' resto, nessuno pone in dubbio, e terminare con la preghiera rituale: e sarebbe forse una viltà poichè il recitare una litania non è un'indagine filosofica. Il perno del problema è altrove. Bisogna vedere che cosa veramente significhi il rinascimento in quanto riguarda la letteratura e verso quale fine, lieta o tragica, ci conduca. Il rinascimento, per dirla in poche parole, ha messo il giornalista nella cattedra del monaco: vale a dire, ha deposto una mentalità acuta, limitata e formale per dare lo scettro ad una mentalità facile ed estesa (come si suol dire nei giornali teatrali), una mentalità irrequieta ed alquanto amorfa. Shakespeare e Lope de Vega sono responsabili, fino ad un certo punto, per il cinematografo. L'instancabile forza creatrice, la calda e viva passionalità, il desiderio intenso di vedere e di sentire, la curiosità sregolata e diffusa degenerano dopo tre secoli in un sensazionalismo frettoloso. Si potrebbe dire infatti dell'uomo moderno che ha un'epidermide invece di un'anima. Il potere sensorio del suo organismo si è enormemente sviluppato ma si è sviluppato a pregiudizio della facoltà spirituale. Il senso morale e forse anche la forza d'immaginazione ci mancano. Le opere letterarie più caratteristiche che possediamo sono semplicemente amorali: *La Crisi* di Marco Praga, *Pelléas et Mélisande* di Maeterlinck, *Crainquebille* d'Anatole France, *Fumée* di Turgenev. Forse le avrò prese piuttosto a vanvera. Non monta: bastano per documentare la tesi che sostengo. Un grande artista moderno volendo musicare il sentimento dell'amore riproduce, per quanto la sua arte glielo permetta, ogni pulsazione, ogni tremito, il più lieve brivido, il più lieve sospiro; gli accordi s'intrecciano e si fanno guerra sorda: si ama mentre s'incrudelisce, si soffre quando e quanto si gode, l'ira ed il dubbio lampeggiano negli occhi degli amanti i cui corpi sono una carne sola. Mettete *Tristano ed Isolta* accanto all' *Inferno* e v'accorgerete come l'odio del poeta segue la sua strada d'abisso in abisso nella scia di un idea che s'intensifica e più intensamente il poeta si consuma nel fuoco dell'idea dell'odio più truce diventa l'arte colla quale l'artista ci comunica la sua passione. L'una è un'arte di circostanze, l'altra è ideativa. Il compilatore d'atlanti nel alto medioevo non si scomponeva quando si trovava in imbarazzo. Scriveva sulla tratta dubbiosa le parole: *Hic sunt leones*. Gli bastava l'idea della solitudine, il terrore delle strane bestie, l'ignoto. La nostra coltura ha tutt'un altro scopo: siamo avidi di dettagli. Il nostro gergo letterario, per questo motivo, non parla che di colore locale, dell'ambiente, dell'atavismo: onde la ricerca febbrile del nuovo e dello strano, l'accumulazione di dettagli osservati o letti, l'ostentazione della coltura generale.

Il rinascimento a rigor di termini dovrebbe significare una nascita dopo una morte, una fecondità improvisa come quella di Sara dopo un lungo periodo di sterilità. Difatti, il rinascimento venne quando l'arte periva di perfezione formale ed il pensiero si perdeva in sottigliezze oziose. Un poema s'era ridotto un problema algebraico, posto e risolto secondo i regolamenti in simboli umani. Un filosofo era un sofista erudito come il Bellarmino o come Giovanni Mariana che, pur predicando al volgo la parola di Gesù, s'arrabbattava a costruire la difesa morale del tirannicidio.

In mezzo a quest'afa il rinascimento entra come un uragano ed in tutta Europa sorge un tumulto di voci e quantunque i cantori non ci siano più le loro opere sono come le conchiglie marine nelle quali, se porgiamo l'orecchio, udiamo riverberare la voce del mare.

Pare, a sentirla, un pianto: o almeno il nostro spirito l'interpreta così. Strana cosa davvero! Tutta la conquista moderna, dell'aria, della terra, del mare, della malattia, dell'ignoranza, si fonde, per così dire, nel crogiulo della mente e si trasforma in una piccola goccia d'acqua, in una lagrima. Se il rinascimento non avesse fatto altro, avrebbe fatto molto creando in noi stessi e nella nostra arte il senso della pietà per ogni essere che vive e spera e muore e s'illude. In questo almeno superiamo gli antichi: in questo il giornalista volgare è più grande del teologo.

James Joyce

"THE UNIVERSAL
LITERARY INFLUENCE
OF THE RENAISSANCE"

The theory of evolution, in the light of which our society
basks, teaches us that when we were little we were not yet
grown up. Hence, if we consider the European Renaissance as a
dividing line, we must come to the conclusion that humanity up
to that epoch possessed only the soul and body of a youth, and
only after that epoch did it develop physically and morally to
the point of meriting the name of adult. It is quite a drastic
conclusion, and not very convincing. In fact (if I were not afraid
to seem a *laudator temporis acti*) I should like to attack it with
drawn sword. The much-trumpeted progress of this century
consists largely of a heap of machines the very purpose of
which is to gather in haste and fury the scattered elements of
utility and knowledge and to redistribute them to each member
of the collectivity who is in a position to pay a slight tax. I
admit that this social system can boast of great mechanical conquests and great beneficial discoveries. It suffices, to be con-
vinced of it, to make a brief list of what may be seen in the
streets of a modern city: the electric tram, telegraph wires, the
humble and necessary postman, the newsboys, the large commercial businesses, etc. But in the midst of this complex and

many-sided civilization the human mind, almost terrified by materialistic vastness, is bewildered, forsakes itself, and withers. Must we then come to the conclusion that present-day materialism—which descends in a straight line from the Renaissance—atrophies the spiritual faculties of man, hampers their development, and dulls their refinement? Let us see.

At the time of the Renaissance the human spirit struggled against scholastic absolutism, against that immense (and in many respects admirable) philosophical system which has its deepest foundations in Aristotelian thought, cold, clear, and intrepid, while its summit rises to the attractive and mysterious light of Christian ideology. But if the human spirit struggled against this system, it was not because the system itself was foreign to it. The yoke was sweet and light: but it was a yoke. So that when the great rebels of the Renaissance proclaimed the good news to the European peoples that tyranny no longer existed, that human wretchedness and suffering had vanished like fog in the rising sun, that man was no longer a prisoner, the human spirit perhaps experienced the fascination for the unknown; heard the voice of the visible, tangible, inconstant world, where one lives and dies, sins and repents; and, abandoning the cloistered peace in which it languished, embraced the new gospel. It abandoned its peace, its true abode, because it had grown tired of it, much as God, tired (may my somewhat irreverent observation be forgiven) of his divine perfections, calls forth creation from the void; as a woman, tired of the peace and quiet that distress her heart, turns her gaze toward the temptations of life. Giordano Bruno himself says that every power, whether in nature or in the spirit, must create an opposite power, without which it cannot fulfill itself, and he adds that in each such separation there is a tendency toward reunion. The dualism of the sublime Nolan reflects faithfully the phenomenon of the Renaissance. And if it seems a little arbitrary to quote a witness against himself, to quote the exact words of an innovator to condemn (or at least to judge) the work of which he was the author, I answer that I am doing nothing more than following the example of Bruno himself, who in his long and persistent and captious self-defense turns the weapons of the accusation against the accuser.

It would be easy to fill these pages with the names of the great writers whom the wave of the Renaissance carried up to the clouds (or thereabouts), to praise the grandeur of their works, which, however, no one doubts, and to finish with the ritual prayer; and perhaps it would be a cowardly thing to do since reciting a litany is not a philosophical inquiry. The pivot of the problem is elsewhere. We must see what the Renaissance really means with respect to literature and to what end, joyful or tragic, it leads us. The Renaissance, to be concise, has put the journalist in the monk's chair: that is to say, has deposed an acute, limited and formal mentality to give the scepter to a mentality that is facile and wide-ranging (in the parlance of theater journals), a restless and rather amorphous mentality. Shakespeare and Lope de Vega are responsible, to a certain point, for cinematography. The untiring creative force, the hot and lively passionate temperament, the intense desire to see and sense, and excessive and diffuse curiosity degenerate after three centuries into frenetic sensationalism. We might say indeed that modern man has an epidermis rather than a soul. The sensory power of his body has developed enormously, but it has developed to the detriment of the spiritual faculty. We lack moral sense and perhaps also strength of imagination. The most characteristic literary works we possess are simply amoral: *The Crisis* of Marco Praga, *Pelléas et Mélisande* of Maeterlinck, *Crainquebille* of Anatole France, and *Smoke* of Turgenev. Perhaps I have taken them rather at random. It does not matter: they suffice to document my thesis. A great modern artist wishing to put the senti-

ment of love to music reproduces, as far as his art permits, each
pulsation, each trembling, the lightest shivering, the lightest sigh;
the harmonies intertwine and oppose each other secretly: one
loves even as one grows more cruel, suffers when and as much as
one enjoys, hate and doubt flash in the lovers' eyes, their bodies
become one single flesh. Place *Tristan und Isolde* next to the
Inferno and you will notice how the poet's hate follows its
path from abyss to abyss in the wake of an idea that intensifies;
and the more intensely the poet consumes himself in the fire
of the idea of hate, the more violent becomes the art with
which the artist communicates his passion. One is the art of
circumstance, the other is ideational. The compiler of atlases
in the high middle ages did not lose his composure when he was
in a quandary. He would write on the doubtful area the words:
Hic sunt leones. The idea of solitude, the terror of strange beasts,
the unknown were quite sufficient for him. Our culture has
an entirely different outlook; we are avid for details. Our literary slang, for this reason, speaks only of local color, ambience
and atavism: whence the feverish search for the new and the
strange, the accumulation of observed or read details, the osten-
tation of the general culture.

The Renaissance in the strict sense should signify a birth
after a death, an unexpected fecundity like that of Sarah after
a long period of sterility. In truth, the Renaissance occurred
when art was perishing from formal perfection and thought was
lost in idle subtleties. A poem was reduced to an algebraic problem, considered and resolved according to regulations in human
symbols. A philosopher was an erudite sophist like Bellarmine
or like Giovanni Mariana who, while yet preaching the word of
Jesus to the masses, endeavored to construct a moral defense for
tyrannicide.

The Renaissance entered like a hurricane into the center of
this doldrum, and a tumult of voices arose throughout Europe;

and although the singers are gone, their works are like seashells in which, if we place them to the ear, we may hear the sea reverberate.

It seems, upon hearing it, a lament: or at least our spirit interprets it so. A strange thing indeed! All the modern conquests of the air, the earth, the sea, disease, ignorance, are dissolved, so to speak, in the crucible of the mind and are transformed into a drop of water, into a tear. If the Renaissance did nothing else, it would have done much in creating in ourselves and in our art the sense of compassion for each thing that lives and hopes and dies and deludes itself. In this at least we surpass the ancients: in this the ordinary journalist is greater than the theologian.

James Joyce

Translated by
Louis Berrone

R. UNIVERSITÀ DEGLI STUDI DI PADOVA

The Centenary of Charles Dickens.

The influence which Dickens has exercised on the English language (second perhaps to that of Shakespeare alone) depends to a large extent on the popular character of his work. Examined from the standpoint of literary art or even from that of literary craftsmanship he hardly deserves a place among the highest. The form he chose to write in, diffuse, overloaded with minute and often irrelevant observation, carefully relieved at regular intervals by the unfailing humorous note, is not the form of the novel which can can carry the greatest conviction. Dickens has suffered not a little from too ardent admirers. Before his centenary there was perhaps a tendency to decry him somewhat. Towards the close of the Victorian period the peace of literary England was disturbed by the inroads of Russian and Scandinavian writers inspired by artistic ideals very different from those according to which the literary works (at least of the last century) of the chief writers of fiction had been shaped. A fierce and headstrong

(1

earnestness, a resoluteness to put before the
reader the naked, nay, the flayed and
bleeding reality, coupled with a rather
puerile desire to shock the prim
middle-class sentimentalism of those
bred to the Victorian way of thinking
and writing — all these startling qualities
combined to overthrow, or perhaps it would
be better to say, to depose the standard
of taste. By comparison with the stern
realism of Tolstoy, Zola, Dostrievsky, Bjornson
and other novelists of ultra-modern
tendency the work of Dickens seemed
to have paled, to have lost its freshness.
Hence, as I have said, a reaction set in
against him and so fickle is popular
judgment in literary matters that he
was attacked almost as unduly as
he had been praised before. It is
scarcely necessary to say that his
proper place is between these two
extremes of criticism; he is neither
the great-hearted, great-brained,
great-souled writers in whose honour
his devotees burn so much incense
nor yet the common purveyor of
sentimental domestic drama and
emotional claptrap as he appears
to the jaundiced eye of a critic
of the new school.

He has been nicknamed "the
great Cockney": no epithet could describe
him more neatly and nor more fully. Whenever
he went far afield to America (as in

American Notes) or to Italy (as in Pictures from Italy) his magic seems to have failed him, his hand seems to have lost her ancient cunning. Anything drearier, and therefore less Dickensian, than the American chapters of Martin Chuzzlewit it would be hard to imagine. If Dickens is to move you, you must not allow him to stray out of hearing of the chimes of Bow Bells. There he is on his native heath and there are his kingdom and his power. The life of London is the breath of his nostrils: he felt it as no writer since or before his time has felt it. The colours, the familiar noises, the very odours of the great metropolis unite in his work as in a mighty symphony wherein humour and pathos, life and death, hope and despair, are inextricably interwoven. We can hardly appreciate this now because we stand too close to the scenery which he described and are too intimate with his amusing and moving characters. And yet it is certainly by his stories of the London of his own day that he must finally stand or fall. Even Barnaby Rudge though the scene is laid chiefly in London and though it contains certain pages not unworthy of being placed beside the Journal of the Plague of Defoe (a writer, I may remark incidentally, of much

greater importance than is commonly
supposed) does not show us Dickens
at his best. His realm is not the London
of the time of Lord George Gordon but
the London of the time of the Reform Bill.
The provinces indeed, the English country
of "meadows trim with daisies pied,"
appear in his work but always as a
background or as a preparation. With
much greater truth and propriety could
Dickens have applied to himself Lord
Palmerston's famous Civis Romanus sum.
The noble lord, to tell the truth, succeeded
on that memorable occasion (as Gladstone,
unless my memory misleads me, took
care to point out) in saying the opposite
of what he had in mind to say.
Wishing to say that he was an
imperialist he said that he was
a Little Englander. Dickens, in fact, is
a Londoner in the best and fullest sense
of the word. The church bells which rang
over his dismal, squalid childhood,
over his struggling youth, over his
active and triumphant manhood, seem
to have called him back whenever,
with scrip and wallet in his hand,
he intended to leave the city and
to have bidden him turn again, like
another Whittington, promising him
(and the promise was to be amply
fulfilled) a threefold greatness. For
this reason he has a place for ever
in the hearts of his fellow-citizens

4)

R. UNIVERSITÀ DEGLI STUDI DI PADOVA

and also for this reason the legitimate
affection of the great city for him has
coloured to no slight extent the criticisms
passed upon his work. To arrive at a
just appreciation of Dickens, to estimate
more accurately his place in what we
may call the national gallery of
English literature it would be well
to read not only the eulogies of the
London-born but also the opinions of
representative writers of Scotland, or the
Colonies or Ireland. It would be interesting
to hear an appreciation of Dickens
written, so to speak, at a proper focus
from the original by writers of his
own class and of a like (if somewhat
lesser) stature, near enough to him in
aim and in form and in speech to
understand, far enough from him in
spirit and in blood to criticise. One is
curious to know how the great Cockney
would fare at the hands of R. L. S.
or of Mr Kipling or of Mr George Moore.

Pending such final judgment we
can at least assign him a place among
the great literary creators. The number
and length of his novels prove incontestably
that the writer is possessed by a kind

(5

of creative fury. As to the nature of the work so created we shall be safe if we say that Dickens is a great caricaturist and a great sentimentalist, (using those terms in their strict sense and without any malice) — a great caricaturist in the sense that Hogarth is a great caricaturist, a sentimentalist in the sense which Goldsmith would have given to that word. It is enough to point to a row of his personages to see that he has few (if any) equals in the art of presenting a character, fundamentally natural and probable with just one strange, wilful, wayward moral or physical deformity, which upsets the equipoise and bears off the character from the world of tiresome reality and as far as the borderland of the fantastic. I should say perhaps the human-fantastic for what figures in literature are more human and warm-blooded than Micawber, Pumblechook, Simon Tappertit, Peggoty, Sam Weller (to say nothing of his father), Sara Gamp, Joe Gargery? We do not think of these, and of a host of others in the well-crowded Dickensian gallery, as tragic or comic figures or even as national or local types as we think, for instance, of the characters of Shakespeare. We do not even see them through the eyes of their creator with that quaint spirit of nice and delicate

6)

observation with which we see the pilgrims at
the Tabard Inn, noting, ——(smiling and
indulgent) the finest and most elusive
points in dress or speech or gait. No, we
see every character of Dickens in the light
of one strongly-marked or even exaggerated
moral or physical quality, — sleepiness,
whimsical self-assertiveness, monstrous
obesity, disorderly recklessness, reptile like
servility, intense round-eyed stupidity,
tearful and absurd melancholy. And yet
there are some simple people who
complain that, though they like Dickens
very much and have cried over the
fate of Little Nell and over the death
of poor Joe, the crossing-sweeper, and
laughed over the adventurous caprices
of Pickwick and his fellow-musketeers
and hated (as all good people should)
Uriah Heep and Fagin the Jew, yet
he is after all a little exaggerated. To
say this of him is really to give him
what I think they call in that land
of strange phrases, America, a billet
for immortality. It is precisely this
little exaggeration which rivets his
work firmly to popular taste, which
fixes his characters firmly in popular
memory. It is precisely this little
exaggeration that Dickens has influenced
the spoken language of the inhabitants
of the British Empire as no other
writer since Shakespeare's time has
influenced it and has won for himself

(7

a place deep down in the hearts of his fellow-
countrymen, a honour which has been
withheld from his great rival Thackeray.
And yet is not Thackeray at his finest
greater than Dickens? The question is an
idle one. English taste has decreed to
Dickens a sovereign position and
Turk-like will have no brother
near his throne.

James Joyce B.A.

"THE CENTENARY OF CHARLES DICKENS"

The influence which Dickens has exercised on the English language (second perhaps to that of Shakespeare alone) depends to a large extent on the popular character of his work. Examined from the standpoint of literary art or even from that of literary craftsmanship he hardly deserves a place among the highest. The form he chose to write in, diffuse, overloaded with minute and often irrelevant observation, carefully relieved at regular intervals by the unfailing humorous note, is not the form of the novel which can carry the greatest conviction. Dickens has suffered not a little from too ardent admirers. Before his centenary there was perhaps a tendency to decry him somewhat. Towards the close of the Victorian period the peace of literary England was disturbed by the inroads of Russian and Scandinavian writers inspired by artistic ideals very different from those according to which the literary works (at least of the last century) of the chief writers of fiction had been shaped. A fierce and headstrong earnestness, a resoluteness to put before the reader the naked, nay, the flayed and bleeding reality, coupled with a rather juvenile desire to shock the prim middle-class sentimentalism of those bred to the Victorian way of thinking and writing—all these startling qualities combined to overthrow, or perhaps it would be better to say, to depose the standard of taste. By comparison with the stern realism of Tolstoy, Zola, Dostoiewsky, Bjornson and other novelists of ultra-modern tendency the work of Dickens seemed to have paled, to have lost its freshness. Hence, as I have said, a reaction set in against him and so fickle is popular judgment in literary matters that he was attacked almost as unduly as he had been praised before. It is scarcely necessary to say that his proper place is between these two extremes of criticism; he is neither the great-hearted, great-brained, great-souled writer in whose honour his devotees burn so much incense nor yet the common purveyor of sentimental domestic drama and emotional clap-trap as he appears to the jaundiced eye of a critic of the new school.

He has been nicknamed "the great Cockney": no epithet could describe him more neatly nor more fully. Whenever he went far afield—to America (as in *American Notes*) or to Italy (as in *Pictures from Italy*) his magic seems to have failed him, his hand seems to have lost her ancient cunning. Anything drearier, and therefore less Dickensian, than the American chapters of *Martin Chuzzlewit* it would be hard to imagine. If Dickens is to move you, you must not allow him to stray out of hearing of the chimes of Bow Bells. There he is on his native heath and there are his kingdom and his power. The life of London is the breath of his nostrils: he felt it as no writer since or before his time has felt it. The colours, the familiar noises, the very odours of the great metropolis unite in his work as in a mighty symphony wherein humour and pathos, life and death, hope and despair, are inextricably inter-woven. We can hardly appreciate this now because we stand too close to the scenery which he described and are too intimate with his amusing and moving characters. And yet it is certainly by his stories of the London of his own day that he must finally stand or fall. Even *Barnaby Rudge* though the scene is laid chiefly in London and though it contains certain pages not unworthy of being placed beside the *Journal of the Plague* of Defoe (a writer, I may remark incidentally, of much greater importance than is commonly supposed) does not show us Dickens at his best. His realm is not the London of the time of Lord George Gordon but the London of the time of the Reform Bill. The provinces indeed, the English country of "meadows trim with daisies pied," appear in his work but always as a background or as a preparation. With much greater truth and propriety could Dickens have applied to himself Lord Palmerston's famous *Civis Romanus sum*. The noble lord, to tell the truth, succeeded on that memorable occasion (as Gladstone, unless my memory misleads me, took care to point out) in saying the opposite of what he had in mind to say. Wishing to say that he was an imperialist he said that he was a Little Englander. Dickens, in fact, is a Londoner in the best and fullest sense of the word. The church bells which rang over his dismal, squalid childhood, over his struggling youth, over his active and triumphant manhood, seem to have called him back whenever, with scrip and wallet in his hand, he intended to leave the city and to have bidden him turn again, like another Whittington, promising him (and the promise was to be amply fulfilled) a threefold greatness. For this reason he has a place for ever in the hearts of his fellow-citizens and also for this reason the legitimate affection of the great city for him has coloured to no slight extent the criticisms passed upon his work. To arrive at a just appreciation of Dickens, to estimate more accurately his place in what we may call the national gallery of English literature it would be well to read not only the eulogies of the London-born but also the opinions of representative writers of Scotland, or the Colonies or Ireland. It would be interesting to hear an appreciation of Dickens written, so to speak, at a proper focus from the original by writers of his own class and of a like (if somewhat lesser) stature, near enough to him in aim and in form and in speech to understand, far enough from him in spirit and in blood to criticise. One is curious to know how the great Cockney would fare at the hands of R.L.S. or of Mr Kipling or of Mr George Moore.

Pending such final judgment we can at least assign him a place among the great literary creators. The number and length of his novels prove incontestably that the writer is possessed by a kind of creative fury. As to the nature of the work so created we shall be safe if we say that Dickens is a great caricaturist and a great sentimentalist, (using those terms in their strict sense and without any malice)—a great caricaturist in the sense that Hogarth is a great caricaturist, a sentimentalist in the sense which Goldsmith would have given to that word. It is enough to point to a row of his personages to see that he has few (if any) equals in the art of presenting a character, fundamentally natural and probable with just one strange, wilful, wayward moral or physical deformity which upsets the equipoise and bears off the character from the world of tiresome reality and as far as the borderland of the fantastic. I should say perhaps the human-fantastic for what figures in literature are more human and warmblooded than Micawber, Pumblechook, Simon Tappertit, Peggot[t]y, Sam Weller (to say nothing of his father), Sara Gamp, Joe Gargery? We do not think of these, and of a host of others in the well-crowded Dickensian gallery, as tragic or comic figures or even as national or local types as we think, for instance, of the characters of Shakespeare. We do not even see them through the eyes of their creator with that quaint spirit of nice and delicate observation with which we see the pilgrims at the Tabard Inn, noting, (smiling and indulgent) the finest and most elusive points in

PLATE I
The portico of Il Palazzo del Bo,
University of Padua

PLATE II
Classroom in Il Palazzo del Bo, University of Padua,
possibly the one where Joyce sat for his examinations

PLATE III
Via della Barriera Vecchia 32, Trieste,
where Joyce lived in April 1912

PLATE IV
Nora, Joyce, Lucia and Giorgio,
Trieste

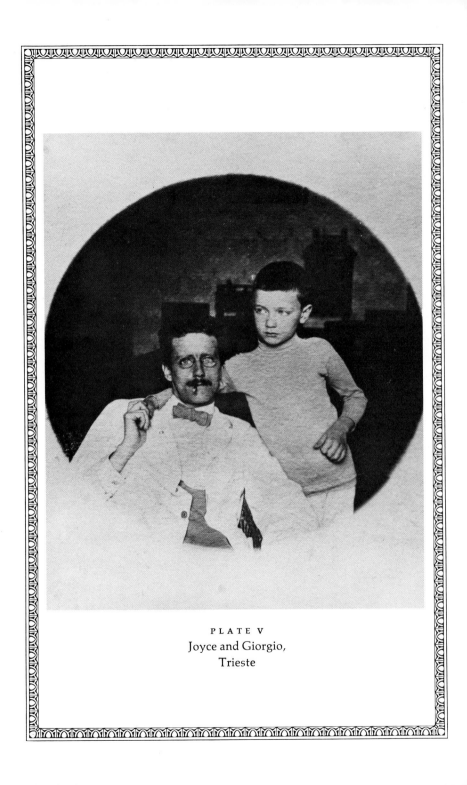

PLATE V
Joyce and Giorgio,
Trieste

PLATE VI

A ninth-century Anglo-Saxon map of the world.
Hic abundant leones
is written above the picture
of a lion in the upper left-hand corner

PLATE VII (2 photographs)
1. St. George's Church and Leopold Bloom's House,
7 Eccles Street, Dublin

2. St. Mary-le-Bow Church (Bow bells),
London

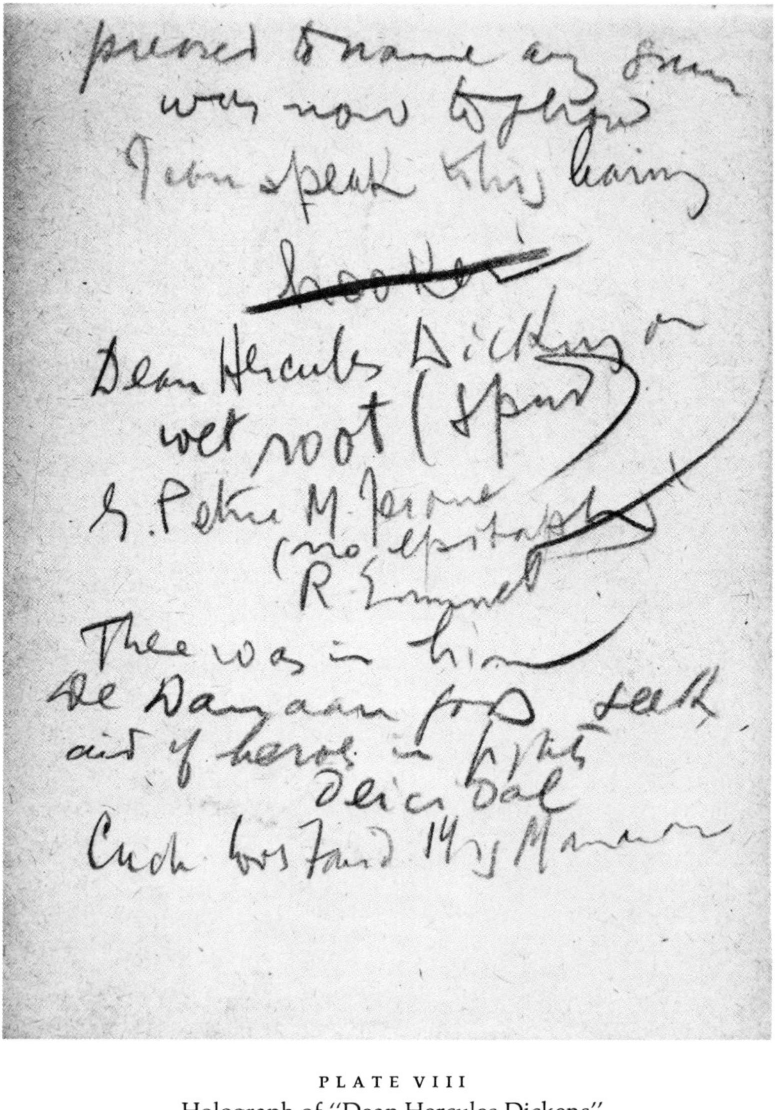

PLATE VIII

Holograph of "Dean Hercules Dickens"
from the *Finnegans Wake Notebook*

dress or speech or gait. No, we see every character of Dickens in the light of one strongly-marked or even exaggerated moral or physical quality—sleepiness, whimsical self-assertiveness, monstrous obesity, disorderly recklessness, reptile-like servility, intense round-eyed stupidity, tearful and absurd melancholy. And yet there are some simple people who complain that, though they like Dickens very much and have cried over the fate of Little Nell and over the death of poor Joe, the crossing-sweeper, and laughed over the adventurous caprices of Pickwick and his fellow-musketeers and hated (as all good people should) Uriah Heep and Fagin the Jew, yet he is after all a *little* exaggerated. To say this of him is really to give him what I think they call in that land of strange phrases, America, a billet for immortality. It is precisely this little exaggeration which rivets his work firmly to popular taste, which fixes his characters firmly in popular memory. It is precisely by this little exaggeration that Dickens has influenced the spoken language of the inhabitants of the British Empire as no other writer since Shakespeare's time has influenced it and has won for himself a place deep down in the hearts of his fellow-countrymen, a honour which has been withheld from his great rival Thackeray. And yet is not Thackeray at his finest greater than Dickens? The question is an idle one. English taste has decreed to Dickens a sovereign position and Turk-like will have no brother near his throne.

James Joyce, B. A.

1912

REGIA UNIVERSITÀ DI PADOVA

PROCESSO VERBALE

DEGLI ESAMI PER L'ABILITAZIONE ALL'INSEGNAMENTO DELLE LINGUE STRANIERE

NEGLI ISTITUTI DI ISTRUZIONE MEDIA DI SECONDO GRADO

secondo il R. Decreto N. 210 del 16 aprile 1908

Sig. *Joyce James* figlio di *Giovanni*

nato a *Dublino* provincia di candidato all'abilitazione per

la lingua *Inglese* ha nei giorni *22, 25, 26 aprile 1912* sostenute

le prove scritte

1° Componimento italiano	punti *trenta*	sopra	50
2° Componimento nella lingua straniera	*cinquanta*		
3° Scrittura sotto dettato	*cinquanta*		
4° Traduzione nella lingua straniera di un brano di autore italiano	*cinquanta*		

Nel giorno *30 Aprile* fu sottoposto agli esami orali ed ottenne:

Nella versione in italiano di qualche passo di poeta o prosatore straniero . punti *quarantasei* sopra 50

Nella versione dall'italiano nella lingua straniera con commento
grammaticale . . . . *cinquanta* .

Nelle risposte nella lingua straniera ed altre interrogazioni di grammatica *cinquanta* .

Nelle risposte in lingua italiana ad interrogazioni di storia della
letteratura straniera . . . . . . *quarantacinque* .

La lezione di prova tenuta nel giorno *30 Aprile* sul tema:

1) The Rise of the Drama 2) The Good Parson di Chaucer

ottenne *cinquanta* sopra **cinquanta**.

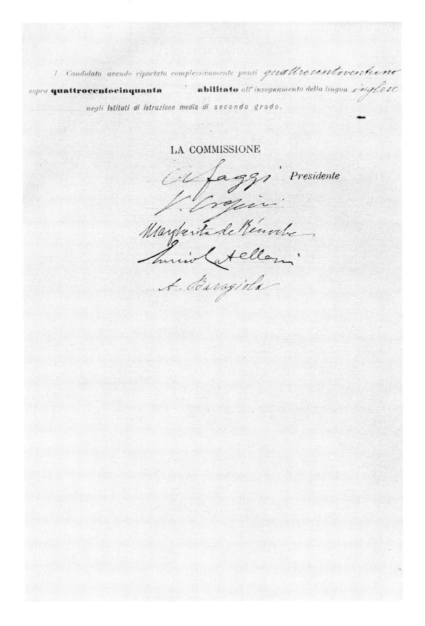

Il Candidato avendo riportato complessivamente punti quattrocentoventuno *sopra* **quattrocentocinquanta** *abilitato all'insegnamento della lingua* inglese *negli Istituti di istruzione media di secondo grado.*

LA COMMISSIONE

Presidente

The University of Padua Official Reports

1912
ROYAL UNIVERSITY OF PADUA

Official Report
of the examinations for the teacher's diploma of foreign languages
in the Institutions of Secondary School Instruction
according to the R. Decree N. 210 of April 16, 1908

Mr._____Joyce James_____son of____John____

born in___Dublin___province of_____candidate for the
diploma of the language__English__has on the days__April 24, 25, 26, 1912__
taken the written tests

1 Italian composition .... points___thirty___out of 50

2 Composition in a foreign language...... "   ___fifty___   " " "

3 Written dictation .... "   ___fifty___   " " "

4 Translation into the foreign language
   of a passage from an Italian author..... "   ___fifty___   " " "

On the day___April 30___was enrolled for the oral examinations
and received:

In the translation into Italian of a passage
of a foreign poet or prose writer........points___forty-six___out of 50

In the translation from Italian into the foreign
language with grammatical commentaries.. "   ___fifty___   " " "

In the answers in the foreign language and
other questions on grammar............ "   ___fifty___   " " "

In the answers in Italian to questions on
the history of the foreign literature....... "   ___forty-five___ " " "

The test lesson given on the day___April 30___on the theme:
1) ___The Rise of the Drama___ 2) ___The Good Parson of Chaucer___
received___fifty___out of fifty.

The candidate having earned a total of <u>four hundred and twenty-</u> <u>one</u> out of four hundred and fifty_____qualified for the teaching of the <u>English</u> language in Institutions of Secondary School of the second degree.

The Commission

AFTERWORD I

―――・―◆―・―――

"THE UNIVERSAL LITERARY INFLUENCE
OF THE RENAISSANCE"

The ancient map-makers wrote across unexplored
regions, "Here are lions."

W. B. Yeats
The Celtic Twilight

Joyce liked to think in terms of opposing forces and recurring
cycles. What has come to pass will be opposed and will pass
away, only to return again, transformed, to be opposed once
more. Though he attacked certain effects of the Renaissance in
his first Padua essay, it was not because he was an inveterate
medievalist but rather because he wished to view the Renaissance and its effects from the perspective of the twentieth
century. He recognized that the Renaissance was a necessary
response to the negative and outworn aspects of the Middle
Ages, but his Jesuit education gave him a scholastic vision of the
world from his earliest years; and he never lost his respect for
what were for him the most positive qualities of that tradition.
Perhaps it was because he was so aware of these qualities that
he resisted the idea that medieval culture was immature when
compared with that of the Renaissance.

At the beginning of the essay Joyce rejects the idea that
the soul of humanity before the Renaissance was juvenile, and
that only afterwards did it evolve into physical and moral matur-
ity. A mind attuned to observe opposing forces and recurring
cycles would not easily concede the point that the inner life

of man was evolving in linear, successive steps. Some modern materialistic effects of the Renaissance represent in Joyce's eyes a step backward for the soul, rather than its advancement. He views twentieth-century progress largely as a heap of machines, furiously gathering and redistributing "the scattered elements of utility and knowledge." There have been mechanical conquests and discoveries; but in "this complex and many-sided civilization the human mind, almost terrified by materialistic vastness, is bewildered, forsakes itself, and withers." Materialism, descending directly from the Renaissance, weakens the spiritual life, hampers its growth, and dulls its refinement.

In the break from scholastic absolutism, there was a promise of freedom from tyranny and suffering; and "the human spirit . . . heard the voice of the visible, tangible, inconstant world," and reacted against medieval values in a manner defined by the Renaissance Italian philosopher, Giordano Bruno. In Joyce's words, Bruno "says that every power, whether in nature or in the spirit, must create an opposite power, without which it cannot fulfill itself and . . . that in each separation there is a tendency towards reunion."[1] Joyce had respected Bruno from his student days at University College, Dublin. In this essay he calls Bruno, who was born in Nola, a city near Naples, the "sublime Nolan." One brilliancy in the essay as a whole is its thematic orchestration of opposites throughout, and, incredible as it may sound for an impromptu exam, its *conclusion as a reconciliation*, or at least an approximation of one, in true Bruno style.

There are many great Renaissance writers, but merely to list their accomplishments would be a litany rather than a philosophical inquiry. The focus lies elsewhere. What is the significance of the influence of the Renaissance on literature? It is easy enough to agree with Joyce's assertions concerning the externalizing and sensate effects of the Renaissance—"that modern man has an epidermis rather than a soul." Television's excitations intensify his point. Some critics may quarrel with his blaming the movie industry on Shakespeare's and Lope de Vega's numerous plays and object to his argument as a *post hoc, propter hoc* fallacy. Doing so would be to miss the point of the hyperbole and the overall scope of Joyce's vision.[2] Modern man is in search of a soul; and Joyce, for one, saw that it was not to be found skin deep. He says about modern man that "The sensory power of his body has developed enormously, but it has developed to the detriment of the spiritual faculty."

If the Renaissance and its aftermath were not sources or precedents for depicting the interior life, what were the sources and precedents? If we take Bruno's theory of opposites as a model, the precedents could be from Joyce's personal reaction against the emphasis in literature on external reality alone, and also a return to the spirituality (in its best sense) of pre-Renaissance times, which for Joyce was best characterized by Dante. It is in following this thread of thought that he champions Dante's *Inferno* over Wagner's *Tristan und Isolde*.

Dante's art is *ideativa*. Wagner's is *arte di circostanze*. Wagner's music in *Tristan*, in Joyce's view, reproduces the details of moment-to-moment emotional and physical circumstances. But in the *Inferno* the poet's passion follows in the wake of an *idea* of just punishments for worse and worse evils. The *idea* of solitude, the unknown, or fear of strange beasts was enough for the atlas-maker of the high Middle Ages when he wrote *Hic sunt leones;* whereas, Joyce points out, our culture is "avid for details." Joyce attacks the *romantic temperament* in the works of Wagner (and Maeterlinck) because it dwells on the details of shifting emotional and physical circumstances; he also attacks the *detailed outer realism* of such writers as

Marco Praga, Anatole France and Turgenev, citing them as modern examples of the easy, extensive, restless and amorphous Renaissance mentality.

Joyce's complaint would appear to be clear and direct, but then the powerful closing metaphors of the essay are contrapuntal, and continue to oppose his main thesis and reassert and reoppose it in a Brunonian way. The last two sentences of the essay are indeed in praise of the common journalist who, in deposing the theologian, seemed to be the principal culprit from the outset. Joyce recognized capabilities in the journalist that he had, earlier in 1912, praised in the mystic poet William Blake. Compare the conclusion of the Renaissance essay with this statement from his Trieste lecture on Blake: "To him who had such great pity for everything that lives and suffers and rejoices in the illusions of the vegetable world, for the fly, the hare, the little chimney sweep, the robin, even for the flea, was denied any other fatherhood than spiritual fatherhood. . . ."[3]

Joyce was not making a plea for ivory-tower interests in spiritual values in his Renaissance essay. The "journalist" may not be a Thomas Aquinas; but, in that he could express his sensitivity to the inner states of life and could come close in feeling to Blake's poetry, he would in a sense complement and transcend formal Thomistic inquiry into the nature of the soul. And when we remember that Joyce carried blank slips of paper in his pockets to jot down his observations and insights, we recognize that there was indeed a journalistic side to him, one that he did not neglect even as he forged ahead as the master stream-of-consciousness novelist of our age.

To return to the opening argument of Joyce's essay, we note that his opinion that the Renaissance was not necessarily a dividing line in social evolution between the mature and the immature mind is remarkably similar to statements he made in the early twenties to Arthur Power. These statements appear in _Conversations with James Joyce_, published in 1974.[4] Walking along the Boulevard St.-Michel—once a center of medieval Paris —discussing Raymond Lully, Duns Scotus and Albertus Magnus, Joyce said (Chapter XII) that the world of these thinkers represented "the true spirit of Western Europe," and that "the Renaissance was an intellectual return to boyhood." He saw the thought of his day returning cyclically to medieval values. Greek and Roman architecture appeared naïve in comparison with Gothic; Joyce preferred the Cathedral of Notre Dame to the neoclassical Madeleine. He was impressed with its amazingly complicated construction, its overlapping planes, flying buttresses, "erupting gargoyles." The architecture of the classical period seemed "over-simple and lacking in mystery" when compared with such magnificent complexities.

According to Power, Ireland, and Dublin itself, are interesting to Joyce because they remain in essence medieval. The pubs around Christ Church remind him of "medieval taverns in which the sacred and the obscene jostle shoulders. . . ." The Irish peasant is insensitive to the art of the Renaissance because his cultural symbols remain medieval. William Butler Yeats's concern with magic, the power of incantations, signs and symbols and even the bawdiness apparent in his later writing establish him as a medievalist. In Joyce's view his own _Ulysses_ is also "medieval but in a more realistic way." Joyce wished to retain the medieval ability to depict the various planes of the human soul in art and literature, but as a modern writer he realized that he must also base his work to a large extent on realism. One of his criticisms of Yeats was that he placed too great an emphasis on the Celtic myths and that he ignored aspects of modern everyday realism that might illuminate the interior life. In _Conversations_ Joyce attacks classicism as well as the amorphous romanticism and outer realism discussed briefly in the examination essay, as he expanded and redefined his attack against the effects of the Renaissance.

We learn from Chapter VI of *Conversations* that Joyce believes that the modern writer is dealing with people who are far more complicated than characters in a Pushkin short story. Today's writers prefer to probe more intimate and unusual relationships, moods and atmospheres. Joyce prefers poetry to "literature," life to imaginatively trumped-up lies. Poetry is the realm of *homo sapiens;* "literature," in the pejorative sense he extends to it (similar to the distinction he made in *Stephen Hero* and in his essays on Mangan) is the realm of the "perpetual adolescent." The "new realism" (we even perhaps call it "new *inner* realism") of *Ulysses,* Joyce felt, liberated literature from its classical and romantic shackles. Joyce's criticism of earlier writers for their preoccupation with externals and their inability to think on anything but one plane echoes the major point made in his Renaissance essay: that the effects of the restless Renaissance concern for physical detail degenerates into what he calls "sensate" literary modes—those that assault the senses and obstruct, rather than express, the inner life. In discussing earlier writers such as Pushkin and Tolstoy, whose interests lay for the most part in externals and single planes, Joyce tells Power that "the modern theme is the subterranean forces, those hidden tides which govern everything and run humanity counter to the apparent flood: those poisonous subtleties which envelop the soul, the ascending fumes of sex." The inner life of Turgenev's Liza in *Collection of Gentlemen* (Power's title for the work more commonly known as *A Nest of Gentlefolk*) remains unrevealed. Turgenev, like other classical writers, shows us the pleasant exterior but ignores Liza's innermost springs of behavior and thought.

Joyce later states (Chapter IX) that classical literature does not encompass the mystery surrounding life. Classical literature is objective, modern is subjective; classical, that of the daylight of the personality; modern, the twilight. He seeks a "new fusion between the exterior world and our contemporary selves." Imagination and sex are the eternal qualities and the "formal" life tries to suppress both. In respect to environments or backgrounds, those of the classicists and romantics are unreal for most men and their surroundings.

Joyce deflates idealism in the face of overwhelming reality, but then points out that T. S. Eliot obtains striking effects by contrasting the real and the ideal. Both worlds must be included in the poetic vision, "but the hidden or subconscious world is the most exciting and the modern writer is far more interested in the potential than the actual—in the unexplored and hallucinatory even—than in the well-trodden romantic or classical world."

Joyce reflects a modernist perspective when he tells Power in Chapter II that, as well as the emotional outlook there is "also the intellectual outlook which dissects life, and that is now what interests me most, to get down to the residuum of truth about life, instead of puffing it up with romanticism, which is a fundamentally false attitude. In *Ulysses* I have tried to forge literature out of my own experience, and not out of a conceived idea, or a temporary emotion." This view, modern as Joyce thought it was, still has an affinity with the fusion of ideas and passions he discussed in this 1912 essay when writing about Dante under the rubric of *arte ideativa,* or ideational art.

If Joyce's 1912 essay is forward-looking to his later critical theories (as we can see from what he said to Power in the twenties), it is also a culmination of earlier thought. The essay brings Joyce's understanding of medievalism and the point of view of his aesthetics into focus in terms other than those of St. Aquinas's *integritas, consonantia,* and *claritas* and the ecclesi-

astical epiphany, with which we are so familiar from *Stephen
Hero* and *A Portrait*. We recognize that Joyce's preference for
Dante's ideational art over Wagner's art of circumstance is
linked with his admiration for Blake and the symbolist poets.
Ideational art evokes the underlying idea of a passion or of a
physical event; every hair split by circumstances does not have
to be counted.

Joyce gave his Blake–Defoe lectures under the title "Verismo
et idealismo nella letteratura inglese (Daniel Defoe–William
Blake)" at the Università Populare Triestina in early March
1912.[5] He recognized that Blake's feelings were coordinated by
ideas. In his Blake lecture of 1912, where Joyce distinguishes
Blake from Paracelsus and Behmen who influenced him, Joyce
says:

> Blake naturally belongs to another category, that of the
> artists, and in this category he occupies, in my opinion, a unique
> position, because he unites keenness of intellect with mystical
> feeling. This first quality is almost completely lacking in mystical
> art. St. John of the Cross, for example, one of the few idealist
> artists worthy to stand with Blake, never reveals either an innate
> sense of form or a coordinating force of the intellect in his book
> *The Dark Night of the Soul*, that cries and faints with such an
> ecstatic passion.[6]

Two planes, ideas and emotions are present in Blake; in St. John
of the Cross there is only one, "ecstatic passion," even as
Wagner's romantic music—to move from sublime circumstantial
art to the erotic—is also on one plane.

Joyce most probably drew upon his earlier comments on
Blake for his analysis of Dante's art as ideational and his point
that the poet's *hatred* follows in the *wake of an idea* in the
Inferno. That Joyce recognized an affinity between Blake and
Dante is apparent in the Blake lecture: he relates how Blake in

his old age "began to study Italian in order to read the *Divina Commedia* in the original and to illustrate Dante's vision with mystical drawings."[7] Joyce imagined Blake's uniting "keenness of intellect with mystical feeling" in his drawings for *The Divine Comedy*. Also, although the example of the art of circumstance that Joyce uses in the Renaissance essay, namely Wagner's music in *Tristan*, is remote in subject and theme from St. John's *Dark Night of the Soul*, we can see how, by way of Joyce's aesthetic views, it is analogous in its tracings of the lovers' sighs and tremblings with St. John's tracing of the "cries and faints" of his passion.

Joyce discusses ideational art in an indirect but revealing way in his Blake lecture. This lecture would seem to have been a partial source for his concept of ideational art in his Renaissance essay and a bridge back to a deeper source in Yeats's essays in *Ideas of Good and Evil* (1896–1903). The ideas that lead to his specific use of the word *ideational* in the Blake lecture are also used in the Padua essay of 1912. In defending Blake against accusations of madness because he did not believe in a precipitous materialism, Joyce sees an opposition between artists, theologians, and philosophers on the one hand, and photographers and court stenographers on the other. This opposition parallels that between the monk and the journalist he mentions in the Renaissance essay.

In the Blake lecture Joyce says, "Such a slaughter of the innocents would take in a large part of the peripatetic system, all of medieval metaphysics, a whole branch of the immense symmetrical edifice constructed by the Angelic Doctor, St. Thomas Aquinas, Berkeley's idealism, and (what a combination) the scepticism that ends with Hume. With regard to art, then, those very useful figures, the photographer and court stenographer, would get by all the more easily."[8] He goes on to say that he does not think that Blake is a great mystic because his works, like those of all Western mystics, shine with a light reflected from oriental thought: "(if that ideational energy that created the vast cycles of spiritual activity and passivity of which the *Upanishads* speak can be called thought)."[9]

Mason and Ellmann translate Joyce's Italian phrase "*energia ideativa*"[10] as "ideational energy" in the above quotation; I have followed them in translating *ideativa* in the phrase "*arte ideativa*" in the Renaissance essay as *ideational*. Joyce's phrase *arte ideativa* of April 1912 is partially derived from the phrase *energia ideativa*, which occurs in his Blake lecture of March 1912. *Energia ideativa* is in turn quite close to and probably partially derived from Blake's phrase "imaginative energy." Yeats uses this expression to identify the power behind the procession of symbols in Blake's poetry in his essay "Symbolism in Painting" (1898) in *Ideas of Good and Evil*:

> A Keats or a Calvert is as much a symbolist as a Blake or a Wagner; but he is a fragmentary symbolist, for while he evokes in his persons and his landscapes an infinite emotion, a perfected emotion, a part of the Divine Essence, he does not set his symbols in the great procession as Blake would have him, "in a certain order, suited" to his "imaginative energy."[11]

In his Blake lecture Joyce focuses on the effectiveness of *energia ideativa* to create the vast cycles in the mystic poetry of the *Upanishads*, even as Yeats before him had focused on Blake's "imaginative energy" to give order to his visions as a "systematic mystic." In the Renaissance essay Joyce focuses on Dante's *arte ideativa*, through which he envisages an emotion following in the wake of an idea that intensifies as the poet descends through deeper and deeper abysses in the *Inferno*. It is the idea working in conjunction with emotion that creates or preserves order.

Joyce may have adapted the crux of this point from Yeats's "The Symbolism of Poetry," a companion essay to "Symbolism in Painting," in which Yeats pays his respects to Arthur Symons, the dean of English symbolist aestheticism, whom I shall consider in more detail later. Yeats's view, as cited in this essay, seems to clarify Joyce's remarks on Dante. Yeats says: "It is the intellect that decides where the reader shall ponder over the procession of the symbols, and if the symbols are merely emotional, he gazes from amid the accidents and destinies of the world; but if the symbols are intellectual too, he becomes himself a part of pure intellect, and he is himself mingled with the procession."[12] Joyce's lines concerning Dante and Wagner in his Renaissance essay become somewhat more lucid if considered in the light of the above passage. To be "mingled with" or to be "consumed" in the fire of intellectual envisionings of emotion is a higher order of art for both Yeats and Joyce. Joyce attacks Wagner's *Tristan* specifically as art of circumstance because the composer's music, to his ear, springs from the emotions alone. It would be as though, to express Joyce's thoughts in Yeats's words, Wagner's "symbols are merely emotional," because "he gazes from amid the accidents and destinies of the world."

Perhaps in studying Yeats's writings on Blake for his own Blake lecture of March 1912, Joyce also armed himself with Yeatsian critical precepts upon which he could immediately draw for his examination essay written in Padua in April of the same year.[13] His criticism of *Tristan* does sound like an echo of Yeats's comment in his essay "Blake's Illustrations to Dante" against the dwelling "over-fondly upon any softness of hair or flesh."[14] Yeats quotes Blake to counter this tendency to fall into the least permanent and least characteristic qualities of art: " 'The great and golden rule of art, as well as of life, is this: that the more distinct, sharp and wiry the bounding line, the more perfect the work of art. . . .' "[15] Without the bounding line, the limited and formal sensibility that Joyce admired in his

Renaissance essay, the artist's work would approach, in the Joycean sense, the journalist's and would be "facile and wide-ranging . . . restless and rather amorphous." Without the bounding line that would focus on what is permanent and most characteristic, in Yeats's words, "you must needs imitate with a languid mind the things you saw or remembered, and so sink into the sleep of nature where all is soft and melting."[16] After even such a brief glimpse into the subtleties of both Joyce's and Yeats's ideational and symbolist aesthetics we see clearly how their work blossomed into truth and beauty from Blakean and Dantesque roots.

But there were other roots as well. Joyce discreetly drew critical sustenance not only from Yeats but also from Yeats's close friend Arthur Symons. Symons dedicated his influential book, *The Symbolist Movement in Literature*,[17] to Yeats, who discussed it in his essay "The Symbolism of Poetry." It was Yeats's collaboration and friendship that earned him Symons's personal dedication. Yeats had introduced Joyce to Symons in London in 1902, and they maintained a consistently cordial and mutually helpful correspondence. In May 1907 Symons successfully aided Joyce in his efforts to publish *Chamber Music*, which Symons reviewed favorably on publication.

As a symbolist poet, critic, and translator of French symbolist poetry, as well as of the poetry and plays of one of Joyce's favorite authors, Gabriele D'Annunzio, Symons was an impressive literary figure. It is not therefore surprising that the development of Joyce's inner-centered symbolist aesthetic views were nurtured by his friendship with Symons; nor was it unexpected that some facets of these views should surface in his Renaissance essay.

Joyce's discussion of ideational art with reference to the medieval atlas-makers in the same essay reflect some of Symons's views on French symbolist aesthetics. Compare the *Hic sunt leones* passage in the Renaissance essay with Symons's comments on Mallarmé in *The Symbolist Movement in Literature,* which was published in 1899 and which Joyce read in the same year:

> Remember his principle: that to name is to destroy, to suggest is to create. Note, further, that he [Mallarmé] condemns the inclusion in verse of anything but, "for example, the horror of the forest, or the silent thunder afloat in the leaves; not the intrinsic, dense wood of the trees."[18]

Symons's quotation is a translation from Mallarmé's *Crise de Vers;* he uses it again in a more amplified context in the same chapter.

Mallarmé's art, like medieval art and that of Joyce himself, is *suggestive.* David Hayman in *Joyce et Mallarmé* points out that Symons himself in the epilogue of *Joyce Book* (1932) relates Joyce to the symbolists, and cites the amplified quotation from *Crise de Vers* that Joyce copied into his Trieste Notebook as evidence of the connection.[19] Hayman also observes that Joyce copied the quotation in French. Joyce thought enough of the French poet and critic to copy him in the original. As *Hic sunt leones*—Here are lions—in the essay conveys both an idea and an emotion, so does Mallarmé's *l'horreur de fôret;* so also does Dante's dark forest *(selva oscura)* in the *Inferno,* where the poet finds himself in the middle of the pathway of his life. If the symbolist movement were to design a coat of arms that would combine Joyce's view of medieval or Dantesque ideational art with that of the symbolists, the design could well be based on an imaginary fusion of metaphors, such as *"Hic sunt leones* in the horror of the dark forest in the middle of the pathway of my life."

And Joyce himself did encounter lions in his pathways

through real and terrible forests. One was Michael Lennon, a Dublin judge with whom Joyce believed himself to be on friendly terms for several years. But in March 1931 Lennon published an article in the American periodical *Catholic World* that slurred Joyce and his family.[20] Other "lions" attacked him in print, either openly or anonymously. He feared that others might harm him if he returned to Ireland. His friends and family urged him to return; but in a letter to Constantine Curran on August 6, 1937, he explains that he cannot take any chances with his countrymen until he finishes *Finnegans Wake*. About Lennon he says, "And on the map of their island there is marked very legibly for the moment Hic sunt Lennones."[21] Joyce also puns on the expression *Hic sunt leones* in *Finnegans Wake*, Part 1, Chapter vii; this time in a pure Mallarméan poetic context that is suggestive in a creative way of the critical precept that it represents. When introvert artist Shem ventures out of seclusion after the War to observe the fairer sex, he finds himself facing a gun:

> . . . he got the charm of his optical life when he found himself (*hic sunt lennones!*) at pointblank range blinking down the barrel of an irregular revolver of the bulldog with a purpose pattern, handled by an unknown quarreler who, supposedly, had been told off to shade and shoot shy Shem should the shit show his shiny shnout out awhile to look facts in their face before being hosed and creased (uprip and jack him!) by six or a dozen of the gayboys.[22]

The *hic sunt lennones!* in this context suggests not only Judge Michael Lennon but other lesser-known attackers as well.

The reader may also hear an echo of Symons's Introduction to *The Symbolist Movement in Literature* in Joyce's Renaissance essay. The concluding paragraph of the Introduction reads:

Here, then, in this revolt against exteriority, against rhetoric, against a materialistic tradition; in this endeavor to disengage the ultimate essence, the soul, of whatever exists and can be realized by the consciousness; in this dutiful waiting upon every symbol by which the soul of things can be made visible; literature, bowed down by so many burdens, may at last attain liberty, and its authentic speech. In attaining this liberty, it accepts a heavier burden; for in speaking to us so intimately, so solemnly, as only religion had hitherto spoken to us, it becomes itself a kind of religion, with all the duties and responsibilities of the sacred ritual.[23]

It is not too much to say that Joyce utilized Symons's attack on exteriority and materialism in his own essay. Symons's statement does, moreover, depict an artist's religious outlook on the world similar to that expressed by Stephen in *A Portrait*, when he envisions himself as a "priest of eternal imagination."

Symons's Introduction to the English translation of D'Annunzio's *A Child of Pleasure* (1898) would also appear to have influenced Joyce. Symons prefers poetry to "fiction dealing with circumstance, which is an accident of time, and character, which is an accident of temperament; with society, which is the convention of external intercourse. . . ."[24] Joyce's attack on what he called the art of circumstance does sound very much like an echo of Symons; some lines from Joyce's essay reflect statements made in Symons's Introduction. While praising the poetic qualities of D'Annunzio's prose and the "states of mind" of his novels, Symons at the same time attacks the exterior novel:

The great exterior novels, we may well believe, have been written; the inter-action of man upon man has been at last suffi-ciently described; what remains, eternally interesting, eternally new, is man, the hidden, inner self which sits silent through all our conversation, and may sit blind at its own presence there, not daring to find itself interesting.[25]

This "inner self" is indeed the spiritual life of man, the life Joyce saw buried in the debris of external details that has been part of our legacy from the Renaissance. In *A Portrait* he dared to find Stephen's inner self interesting, refusing to allow it to remain hidden, or silent, or "blind at its own presence." Joyce's epiphany, that "sudden spiritual manifestation, whether in the vulgarity of speech or of gesture or in a memorable phase of the mind itself," as he defines it in *Stephen Hero*,[26] and which he associates with both Aquinas's *claritas* or radiance, and his *quidditas* or essence, is illustrative to some extent of Symons's concept of a "symbol by which the soul of things can be made visible."[27] Joyce's concept of ideational art would seem to be compatible with both Yeats's and Symons's symbolist aesthetics, as well as with Stephen's ecclesiastical metaphor of epiphany insofar as it has the power both to reveal and set free the spiritual faculties of man from their surrounding circumstances.

Joyce in *A Portrait* wanted to get beyond the external realism, the amorphous details and presentation that he probably felt had vitiated *Stephen Hero*. The need to rewrite *Stephen Hero* was the need to express Stephen's soul from the inside out. Joyce jotted down seventy or more epiphanies for *Stephen Hero* between 1900 and 1903,[28] indicating that he was concerned about spiritual manifestations of life from the earliest stages of the novel. Yet even though he transferred the epiphanies from his Notebooks into *Stephen Hero*, and though Stephen theorizes brightly on them, *Stephen Hero* is not inner-oriented or formally limited. The heavy reliance on diffuse external details, a literary phenomenon Joyce attacked in the Renaissance essay,

prevailed. The heavily factual 231 pages of *Stephen Hero*, show-
ing Stephen in his University days, may be compared with the
93 pages to which they are reduced in *A Portrait*.

Theodore Spencer in his introduction to *Stephen Hero* notes
specific examples of how the wealth of detail in describing people, incidents, and the environment in the first draft almost
vanish in the revision.[29] Objective dramatization gives way to
the focusing of events in Stephen's stream of consciousness. *A
Portrait* thus gains in intensity, concentration and control. A
single point of view rules and makes order out of the scattered
segments of life. Hinting at or suggesting the crux of events
replaces full description. Spencer argues that there is loss as
well as gain in the concentrated version of *A Portrait*. In *Stephen
Hero* Stephen's friends have an independent reality of their
own as they make their appearances or express their views. In
A Portrait they are figures in the landscape of Stephen's mind.
There is no need to identify them beyond giving their names,
expressions and most significant traits. In the depiction of
Stephen's soul the circumstantial details of his friends' lives are
of minor importance. The essential *idea* of who they are and
what they mean to him are paramount; and Spencer's insights
are consistent with Joyce's critical views when he intimates that
these friends do not have to be described fully.

Spencer's view that there is some loss as well as gain in
the final version of *A Portrait*, in that Joyce's friends lose their
independent reality, is true enough. The absence of that kind
of reality to Joyce as an ideational artist would, however,
probably be no greater than the actual loss of his friends in
real life when he left Ireland and recalled them for the most
part as mental states bordering on fiction. Spencer's ideas are
indispensable to an understanding of the transition that took
place in Joyce's own style in November 1907. At that time he

abandoned the *Stephen Hero* manuscript—over a thousand pages long—and started the first three parts of *A Portrait*, which he completed in April 1908.

The extant portion of *Stephen Hero*, that depicting Stephen at the University, had not been rewritten into the last two parts of *A Portrait* at the time Joyce wrote his Renaissance essay. It was still alive in Joyce's mind, and we may recognize some seeds of the ideas that later flowered in the essay and are germane to the revision of *Stephen Hero* are significantly present in *Stephen Hero* itself. In Stephen's essay in *Stephen Hero*, "Art and Life," he discusses the need for the artist to disentangle the soul of an image from exterior qualities. Some of the ideas and the language in Chapter XIX of *Stephen Hero*, while hearkening back to the work of Symons and to Joyce's 1902 and 1907 essays on Mangan, seem to foreshadow the Renaissance essay:

> The artist, he imagined, standing in the position of mediator between the world of his experience and the world of his dreams —"a mediator, consequently gifted with twin faculties, a selective faculty and a reproductive faculty." To equate these faculties was the secret of artistic success: the artist who could disentangle the subtle soul of the image from its mesh of defining circumstances most exactly and "re-embody" it in artistic circumstances chosen as the most exact for it in its new office, he was the supreme artist.[30]

The "mesh of defining circumstances" would seem to be a correlation to Joyce's notion of the art of circumstance discussed in his Paduan essay; and the re-embodiment of "the subtle soul of the image" in *artistic* circumstances would likewise correlate with his notion of ideational art. Stephen's image of the domain of art as cone-shaped is also relevant. The perfect union of the faculty to select from experience and the faculty to reproduce, to re-embody in dreams, was poetry, and thus formed the apex of the cone. The central region of the cone was "literature" and the portraying of externals:

> The term "literature" now seemed to him a term of contempt and he used it to designate the vast middle region which lies between apex and base, between poetry and the chaos of unremembered writing. Its merit lay in its portrayal of externals; the realm of its princes was the realm of the manners and customs of societies—a spacious realm. But society is itself, he conceived, the complex body in which certain laws are involved and over-wrapped and he therefore proclaimed as the realm of the poet the realm of these unalterable laws.[31]

The access to these laws is not the "insecure, unsatisfied, impatient" romantic temper that disregards limitations. It is rather for Stephen in *Stephen Hero* the classical style, "the syllogism of art," that can bridge the world of society and the world of its laws:

> The classical temper on the other hand, ever mindful of limitations, chooses rather to bend upon these present things and to work upon them and fashion them that the quick intelligence may go beyond them to their meaning which is still unuttered.[32]

Joyce's concepts of ideational art and a formal and limited sensibility as expressed in his Renaissance essay seem clearly to suggest the workings of the "quick intelligence" to go beyond "these present things" (external qualities) to their unexpressed meaning. Stephen tries to reconcile "the classical school fighting the materialism that must attend it" and "the romantic school struggling to preserve coherence."[33] And if Stephen is dissatisfied with the romantic temper that can find "no fit abode here for its ideals and chooses therefore to behold them under insensible figures," that produces figures who "are blown to wild adventures, lacking the gravity of solid bodies,"[34] he is also confident that the poetic imagination can transcend the solid embodiments of materialism that are attendant upon classicism.

In expressions that are again suggested in the Renaissance essay he sees the modern machine age from a poetic perspective that rises above materialism. Critics will have to check their calculations with the poet's vision.

> It is time for them to acknowledge that here the imagination has contemplated intensely the truth of being of the visible world and that beauty, the splendour of truth, has been born. The age, though it bury itself fathoms deep in formulas and machinery, has need of these realities which alone give and sustain life and it must await from those chosen centres of vivification the force to live, the security for life which can come to it only from them. Thus the spirit of man makes a continual affirmation.[35]

Some of these points emerge on the first page of the Renaissance essay in a rather more forceful attack against materialism and the machine age; others, such as the poet's penetrating the materialistic maze to contemplate the truth and make affirmation of it, are suggested by Joyce's notion of *arte ideativa* and his stand for the poet's moral imagination.

In the Renaissance essay Joyce attacks some writers of his time for being amoral and unimaginative. This might at first seem strange when one recalls that his own writings were continually attacked as obscene or immoral. Joyce himself in 1934 stated to Bennett Cerf, president of Random House, when *Ulysses* was exonerated by the United States Circuit Court from accusations of obscenity, that at least twenty-two publishers and printers rejected his *Dubliners* manuscript, and, when printed, one person bought out the entire edition and burnt it in Dublin.[36] The bickerings about immorality in Joyce's works have a long history and are still audible today. He himself was concerned about the moral worth of his works from his earliest years as a writer, and his forceful reaction in 1912 to the absence of moral values in literature was not his first. In a fragment of a letter to his brother Stanislaus of July 19, 1905, Joyce worries about being just an entertainer.[37] After reading the Preface and two pages of Oliver Goldsmith's *The Vicar of Wakefield* he had recognized that the social system from which Goldsmith produced his novel was putrid. He thought that Maupassant and contemporary Irish writers were morally obtuse. He himself was determined to live according to his own moral beliefs, even though some people in Ireland might consider such beliefs oblique. Goldsmith in his Preface to *The Vicar*, which launched Joyce into the subject of morality, lauds his hero, the Vicar, as a priest, a husband and as the father of a family. The novel, moreover, shows how the Vicar and his family overcame enormous sufferings. Joyce's wife Nora was nine months pregnant when he wrote the letter, and eight days later Joyce was a father as well as a husband. And if in place of priest we were to substitute artist, which in Joyce's view meant, as Stephen expressed it in *A Portrait*, "priest of eternal imagination," we can see that he was on the mark of the three key virtues of the Vicar's life in his own life as soon as Giorgio was born.

Joyce's view in the Renaissance essay that Marco Praga's *The Crisis*, Maeterlinck's *Pelléas and Mélisande*, Anatole France's *Crainquebille*, and Turgenev's *Smoke* were amoral and unimaginative reflects his distaste for a type of literature in which a strong moral stance and imaginative awareness of underlying human forces were not dramatized in character relationships. The reasons for the amorality and lack of imagination in each of the four works would seem to be diverse.

Praga is an exponent of *verismo*, an Italian kind of naturalism, and the wife in his play *The Crisis* has an adulterous affair out of boredom and for mere sexual gratification; her doting husband blindfolds himself to the affair so as not to lose her.[38] It is a slice-of-life story in which there is a frank discussion of the problems involved.

Crainquebille in France's novel does not have the moral fortitude to withstand imprisonment and ostracism for a crime he never committed (allegedly saying *mortes aux vaches,* "kill the cops," to a cop) and is worn down by imprisonment and public scorn to the depths of drink and degradation.[39] The Russian liberals and political reformers in *Smoke* are hollow men and women.[40] The main characters, Litvinov and Irina, are buffeted back and forth in their love affair by their emotions and are finally separated from each other mainly because Irina cannot free herself from her desire for a place in upper-class society. Joyce probably considered *The Crisis, Crainquebille,* and *Smoke* as realistic portrayals of the submission of individuals to circumstances.

In *Pelléas and Mélisande* the situation is different.[41] Joyce, in this case, may have used Symons's essay "Maeterlinck as Mystic" in *The Symbolist Movement in Literature,* where he comments on Maeterlinck's portrayal of inner states and moods as characters outside the realm of moral concerns. Symons makes the following statement about *Pelléas and Mélisande*:

> I do not know a more passionate love-scene than that scene in the wood beside the fountain, where Pelléas and Mélisande confess the strange burden which has come upon them. When the soul gives itself absolutely to love, all the barriers of the world are burnt away, and all its wisdom and subtlety are as incense poured on a flame. Morality, too, is burnt away, no longer exists, any more than it does for children or for God.[42]

Although Joyce readily accepted symbolist aesthetic principles, he rejected aspects of its morality. And I think we can understand how the fierce Dantean and Ibsenite poet in him would react against the casual manner in which Mélisande gives herself to her husband's brother. The scene might work in Maeterlinck's mystic twilight world of drifting moods and passions, and might titillate the rabblement's prurience, but it was far below Joyce's own standards.[43]

Stephen in *A Portrait* shows moral fiber in the major moments of his formative years, from the time he stands up for his rights against Father Dolan at Clongowes over the issue of his broken glasses to his sticking to his convictions at the university. His morality in his later years is not that of the orthodox Catholicism of his youth, but he is firm in sustaining what he believes to be right and in asserting himself when faced with forces that might threaten to break his spirit. His soul may not conform to orthodox standards, but it remains a soul, powerful, complex and deep-rooted. In spite of the vicissitudes of his life, Stephen remains, like Joyce, true to his moral nature, which, since he is a *young man,* is mainly that of an artist and a student preparing himself to create the as-yet uncreated conscience of his race in literature. And *A Portrait,* like a flower blossoming amidst the mire of its age, does emerge as an imaginative, ideational, symbolist and moral work of art.

Notes

[1] This comment on Bruno echoes those in Joyce's review of J. Lewis McIntyre's *Giordano Bruno,* entitled "The Bruno Philosophy" (1903). See *Critical Writings,* pp. 132–134. "As an independent observer, Bruno, however, deserves high honour. More than Bacon or Descartes must he be considered the father of what is called modern philosophy. His system by turns rationalist and mystic, theistic and pantheistic is everywhere impressed with his noble mind and critical intellect, and is full of that ardent sympathy with nature as it is— *natura naturata*—which is the breath of the Renaissance. In his attempt to reconcile the matter and form of the scholastics—formidable names, which in his system as spirit and body retain little of their metaphysical character—Bruno has hardly put forward an hypothesis, which is a curious anticipation of Spinoza. Is it not strange, then, that Coleridge should have set him down a dualist, a later Heraclitus, and should have represented him as saying in effect: 'Every power in nature or in spirit must evolve an opposite as the sole condition and means of its manifestation; and every opposition is, therefore, a tendency to reunion'?" Mason and Ellmann point out in *Critical Writings,* p. 134, that Joyce "is quoting, with slight variations, a footnote to Essay XIII in Coleridge's *The Friend.* Coleridge anticipated Joyce's interest in both Bruno and Vico."

[2] Joyce's comments here about Shakespeare and Lope de Vega in some ways echo his comments about these two writers in his lecture "Daniel Defoe," of March 1912, in Trieste. He argues that Defoe was the first author to express the English spirit since the Norman Conquest and that he is the father of the English novel. English literature after the Norman Conquest and before Defoe "was at school" to Continental masters. "Shakespeare, with his Titianesque palette, his flow of language, his epileptic passionateness, and his creative fury, is an Italianate Englishman, while the Restoration

theater takes its cue from the Spanish theater, from the works of Calderon and Lope de Vega." "Daniel Defoe," ed. and translated by Joseph Prescott, *Buffalo Studies*, pub. by SUNY at Buffalo, Vol. I, No. 1, 1964, p. 7.

[3] "William Blake," in *The Critical Writings of James Joyce*, ed. by Ellsworth Mason and Richard Ellmann (New York: Viking Press, 1959), p. 219. This book will be referred to in further footnotes as *The Critical Writings*.

[4] *Conversations with James Joyce*, ed. by Clive Hart (London: Millington, Ltd., 1974). References to this book will be designated by chapter numbers preceding cursory quotations, since the chapters are fairly short.

[5] Cf. "William Blake," *op. cit.*, p. 214.

[6] "William Blake," *op. cit.*, p. 221.

[7] *Ibid.*, p. 219.

[8] *Ibid.*, p. 220.

[9] *Idem.*

[10] For the Italian text of the Blake lecture see Cornell MS. No. 45 in Robert Scholes, *The Cornell Joyce Collection* (Ithaca: Cornell University Press, 1961), p. 20.

[11] William Butler Yeats, "Symbolism in Painting" in *Ideas of Good and Evil* in *W. B. Yeats: Essays and Introductions* (New York: Macmillan, 1959), pp. 149–50.

[12] Yeats, *Symbolism in Poetry*, in *W. B. Yeats: Essays and Introductions, op. cit.*, p. 161. See also Yeats's "Discoveries," *op. cit.*, p. 293: "emotion must be related to emotion by a system of ordered images."

[13] Compare the beginning of Joyce's Renaissance essay with Yeats's comments on science and externalities in "The Symbolism of Poetry," *op. cit.*, p. 155: "The scientific movement brought with it a literature which was always tending to lose itself in externalities of all kinds, in opinion, in declamation, in picturesque writing, in word-painting, or in what Mr. Symons has called an attempt 'to build in brick and mortar inside the covers of a book'; and now writers have begun to dwell upon the element of evocation, of suggestion, upon what we call the symbolism in great writers."

[14] Yeats, "Blake's Illustrations to Dante," in *W. B. Yeats: Essays and Introductions, op. cit.*, p. 120.

[15] As quoted by Yeats in "Blake's Illustrations to Dante," *op cit.*, p. 120.

Notes

[16] Yeats, "Blake's Illustrations to Dante," *op. cit.,* p. 120.

[17] Arthur Symons, *The Symbolist Movement in Literature,* with Introd. by Richard Ellmann (New York: E. P. Dutton and Co., Inc., 1958).

[18] *The Symbolist Movement in Literature,* p. 71. As quoted by Symons in *The Symbolist Movement in Literature, op. cit.,* pp. 72–73.

[19] David Hayman, *Joyce et Mallarmé: Stylistique de la Suggestion* (Paris: Lettres Modernes, 1956), Vol. I, p. 28.

[20] See Ellmann, *James Joyce* (New York: Oxford University Press, 1965), p. 655.

[21] As quoted by Richard Ellmann, *James Joyce, op. cit.,* p. 717. In a later letter to Curran, postmarked August 17, 1937, Joyce says: "I see one of your neighbors Mr Lennon has also reached the bench. Another to whom I had the honour of being host and to whom I presented at his request, a signed copy of *Ulysses* after which, in an article in the *Catholic World* U.S.A. he informed the Teagues that I had acquired my 'abundant means' by selling to the British authorities in Rome during the war everything I knew about the Austria which had released me on *parole.* (I was in Switzerland during the war and for 4 years in a lawsuit against the British Consulate in Zurich, a suit I won). So much for Ireland's hearts and hands." *Letters,* ed. by Ellmann (New York: Viking Press, 1966), Vol. II, p. 403. Ellmann explains in a footnote that 4 was a hyperbole for 2 years. In a letter to Harriet Shaw Weaver, November 27, 1931, Joyce also lamented Lennon's article: "It is strange that my presence has this effect and my absence produces a violent reaction. For instance, there has appeared in the *Catholic World* (N.Y.) an article—leader—on me which Colum and his wife say is so vulgar and scurrilous that they will not show it to me. They are both indignant over it. Guess who the writer is. Michael Lennon who helped me so much in the Sullivan affair, who asked me for a signed copy of *Ulysses,* whom I invited [to] Llandudno, whom I entertained with Hughes to dinner and talked with till 1 a.m., who afterwards wrote asking me if I would allow his wife to call on me on her way through Paris etc. *Pourquoi?*" *Letters,* Vol. II, pp. 235–36. See also Vol. II, p. 207, p. 214, p. 240, p. 443 for further references to Lennon. Also *Letters,* ed. by Stuart Gilbert, p. 313 and N.B. p. 390.

[22] James Joyce, *Finnegans Wake* (New York: The Viking Press,

1939, pp. 158–59. Other references to *Finnegans Wake* will be to this edition with page numbers in parentheses.

[23] Symons, Introduction to *The Symbolist Movement in Literature, op. cit.,* p. 5.

[24] Symons, Introduction to Gabriele D'Annunzio's *The Child of Pleasure,* translated by Georgina Harding with verses translated and an Introduction by Arthur Symons (Boston: The St. Botholph Society, 1898), p. x. This Introduction is lengthened and reprinted in Symons, *Studies in Prose and Verse* (London: J. M. Dent and Co., and New York: E. P. Dutton and Co., 1904). See "Gabriele D'Annunzio," pp. 129–42.

[25] *Ibid.,* p. ix. For incisive insights into correlations between *A Portrait* and D'Annunzio's *A Child of Pleasure* see Mary T. Reynolds, "Joyce's Villanelle and D'Annunzio's Sonnet Sequence," *Journal of Modern Literature,* Vol. 5, No. 1, Feb., 1976, pp. 19–45.

[26] James Joyce, *Stephen Hero,* ed. from the Manuscript in the Harvard College Library by Theodore Spencer in a New Edition Incorporating the Additional Manuscript Pages in the Yale University Library and the Cornell University Library, ed. by John J. Slocum and Herbert Cahoon (New York: New Directions, 1963), p. 211.

[27] Symons, Introduction, *The Symbolist Movement in Literature, op. cit.,* p. 5.

[28] Robert Scholes and Richard Kain, collectors and eds. of *The Workshop of Dedalus: James Joyce and the Raw Materials for A PORTRAIT OF THE ARTIST AS A YOUNG MAN* (Evanston, Illinois: Northwestern University Press, 1965), Section I, The Epiphanies: Introductory Note, p. 5.

[29] Theodore Spencer, Introduction, *Stephen Hero, op. cit.,* N.B. pp. 10–16.

[30] *Stephen Hero, op. cit.,* pp. 77–78.

[31] *Ibid.,* p. 78.

[32] *Idem.*

[33] *Ibid.,* p. 79.

[34] *Ibid.,* p. 78.

[35] *Ibid.,* p. 80.

[36] James Joyce, "Letter from Mr. Joyce to the Publisher, Reprinted in 1934 edition by permission of the Author," prescript to *Ulysses* (New York: Random House, 1961), pp. xiii–xv.

[37] James Joyce, *Letters,* Vol. II, pp. 99–100.

Notes

[38] See Marco Praga, *La Crisi* (Milano: Fratelli Treves, Editori, 1904).

[39] See Anatole France, *Crainquebille, Putois, et Riquet* (Paris: Calmann-Lévy, editeurs, n.d.). For an English translation see *The Golden Tales of Anatole France* (New York: Dodd, Mead, and Co., 1926).

[40] See Ivan S. Turgenev, *Smoke,* trans. by Natalie Duddington and introduced by Nikolay Andreyev (London: Dent, and New York: Dutton, Everyman's Library, 1970).

[41] See Maurice Maeterlinck, *Pelléas et Mélisande,* trans. by Erving Winslow with an Intro. by Montrose J. Moses (New York: Thomas Y. Crowell and Co., 1804 and 1908). Moses in his Introduction says: "In this world where there is so much we shall never know, there are many, like Mélisande, who are born, as the Doctor says, 'by chance to die,' and in the end 'she dies by chance.' "

[42] Symons, *The Symbolist Movement in Literature, op. cit.,* p. 87.

[43] See James Joyce, "The Day of the Rabblement," in *Critical Writings,* p. 70.

AFTERWORD II

———◆◇◆———

We may now add Joyce's 1912 essay on Dickens to the testimonials published or orated in that year to honor Dickens's birth on February 7, 1812. Joyce thinks that his influence on the English language (second only to that of Shakespeare) follows from the "popular character of his work." Although Joyce notes the English novelist's violations of artistic norms he had advanced in his Renaissance essay, he does not dwell on them. He moves on through contrasting views of Dickens to some of his most positive accomplishments. He has suffered from ardent and uncritical admirers on one hand, and on the other from the displacement of his literary standards by the new wave of realists (Tolstoy, Dostoievsky, and Bjørnson, among others). In Joyce's view his proper place in literary tradition would fall somewhere between the two schools.

Joyce's balancing of opposing views of Dickens in his second Paduan essay reflects the continuance of a Bruno-like counterpointing and resolution of themes. This ordering of his ideas is circumspect and intelligent; and though there are applications of the method in Joyce's earlier essays, its extension throughout these two indicates some subtle refinements. One reason Joyce could write such lucid essays with so many insights and make critical pronouncements on Dickens (in the style of his Renaissance essay) is that he had, in the forefront of his mind, the Bruno instrument.

The Dickens essay also tells us something about Joyce's

method of creating the Dublin he knew so well and its many unique characters (with, one might add, a Dickensian concern for the common man). The Londoner qualities he sees in Dickens are in some ways comparable to the Dubliner qualities in his own works. Both Joyce and Dickens are primarily city novelists. One of the first visitors who read "The Centenary of Charles Dickens" when it was on exhibit at the Nyselius Library at Fairfield University, Connecticut, remarked, "He's writing about himself!" The reader will naturally wish to qualify this quip; but I think that it does call attention to the affinity Joyce felt for "the great Cockney."

In Chapter IV of *Ulysses* the action moves from the outskirts of Dublin to the city itself. Joyce's comments about Dickens as a city novelist are relevant to the city ambience that Joyce begins to create in this chapter. The reader may sense this when Bloom leaves his apartment for the first time and approaches Larry O'Rourke's pub: "From the cellar grating floated up the flabby gush of porter. Through the open doorway the bar squirted out whiffs of ginger, teadust, biscuitmush" (57).[1]
The life of Dublin is literally and figuratively the breath of Joyce's (and Leopold Bloom's) nostrils, even as London life was for Dickens "the breath of his nostrils." Bloom, like Joyce and Dickens, is a great traveler through daytime and nighttime city streets.

Joyce said, "If Dickens is to move you, you must not allow him to stray out of the hearing of the chimes of Bow Bells"; we might make a similar comment on the most moving parts of Joyce's *Ulysses*, which are set within hearing of the bells of St. George's Church, around the corner from 7 Eccles Street, where the Blooms live. The metaphor of the bells certainly must resonate somewhat more widely for both Dickens and Joyce to include sections of the city not actually within hearing range of the ringing bells. Bloom sees the sun nearing the steeple of

St. George's in his first walk through the streets; and he hears the bells ringing at 8:45 A.M. in his second walk at the end of the chapter, as he thinks about Paddy Dignam's funeral:

> A creak and a dark whirr in the air high up. The bells of George's church. They tolled the hour: loud dark iron.
>
> > *Heigho! Heigho!*
> > *Heigho! Heigho!*
> > *Heigho! Heigho!*
>
> Quarter to. There again: the overtone following through the air, third.
> Poor Dignam! (70)

Church bells or chimes can be heard at other times in the novel. These include the fantasy of St. George's bells (471) and "Midnight chimes from distant steeples" (478) in Chapter XV, "Circe." The latter particularly echo two sentences in the Centenary essay:

> Dickens, in fact, is a Londoner in the best and fullest sense of the word. The church bells which rang over his dismal, squalid childhood, over his struggling youth, over his active and triumphant manhood, seem to have called him back whenever, with scrip and wallet in his hand, he intended to leave the city and to have bidden him turn again, like another Whittington, promising him (and the promise was to be amply fulfilled) a threefold greatness.

In "Circe" the chimes "call" to Bloom, as Joyce says the bells "called" to Dick Whittington and Dickens:

> (*Midnight chimes from distant steeples.*)
> THE CHIMES
> Turn again, Leopold! Lord mayor of Dublin!

BLOOM

(*In alderman's gown and chain.*) Electors of Arran Quay, Inns Quay, Rotunda, Mountjoy and North Dock, better run a tramline, I say, from the cattlemarket to the river. That's the music of the future. That's my programme. *Cui bono?* But our buccaneering Vanderdeckens in their phantom ship of finance . . .

AN ELECTOR

Three times three for our future chief magistrate!

(478)

This fragment from the scene suggests the story of Dick Whittington, who thought he heard the Bow bells of St. Mary-le-Bow Church in Cheapside, the "Cockney" section of London, tell him, "Turn again, Whittington, thrice Lord Mayor of London," when he was running away from the city. Bloom in his fantasy listens to the chimes and becomes Lord Mayor of Dublin; and his stumpings for reforms are similar, in spirit and in fact, to those of Dickens. They also have something in common with the reformist outlook of Joyce himself. Compare Joyce's attack on materialism in the first paragraph of his Renaissance essay with Bloom's speech in the company of the actual mayors of Dublin (479).

When Bloom is "anointed" Leopold I of Ireland, "*Joybells ring in Christ church, Saint Patrick's, George's and gay Malahide*" (482). Malahide, a village nine miles north of Dublin, is the furthest point from Dublin that bells ring, and, at that, they ring only in Bloom's fantasy. Molly hears St. George's bells at 2:45 A.M. in the last chapter, which gives her an idea of how late Bloom got home. Leopold and Molly Bloom's day in Dublin is rung in by St. George's bells and their night is rung out by them. The city ethos suggested by Bow bells in Dickens's work is echoed by St. George's bells in *Ulysses*.

There is a similarity between Joyce's statement that Dickens was a great caricaturist like William Hogarth and

Frank Budgen's point that Joyce's writing in *Ulysses* had the caricaturist quality found in Dickens.[2] Budgen met Joyce in Zurich in 1918, and was one of his closest friends until Joyce's death. He observes in *James Joyce and the Making of ULYSSES* that Joyce's laughter is in many different keys in the novel, and that it is often loud, as is the reader's enjoyment of Shakespeare's and Dickens's caricatures. In the Centenary essay Joyce, who is ordinarily chary in his praise of other authors, assigns Dickens "a place among the great literary creators." Surrounded by qualifying statements and showering superlatives, his high estimate of Dickens's *creative power* is a point that might easily be lost. The superlatives sound like those of G. K. Chesterton in *Charles Dickens: A Critical Study* (1906).[3] Chesterton begins his book with an investigation of what it means to be "great" and then attributes "greatness" profusely to Dickens as a man and to his works (the 1942 reprint of the book, with a preface by Alexander Woolcott is, in fact, entitled *Charles Dickens: The Last of the Great Men*). But Chesterton reserves his highest praise for the literary characters created by Dickens who have become immortal. His characters are not mere imitations of real people, they have a unique literary existence.

In his essay "Drama and Life" (1900) Joyce thought that Pumblechook, the corn-chandler in *Great Expectations*, was not the "human and warm-blooded" personage he described in the Centenary essay, but rather a wooden one.[4] Twelve years earlier Joyce had been impressed by the new school of realists under whose intense and revealing gaze the works of both Dickens and Shakespeare lost much of their fascination for many critics and writers. Joyce never entirely lost his respect for the realists; but it is interesting to see that in 1912 he reappraises his appreciation of Dickens's characters who, because they are a *little* exaggerated are fixed "firmly in the popular memory" and have "a billet for immortality."

If we consider the "row of personages" in *Ulysses* we can see that Joyce himself is one of the few equals of Dickens

in the art of presenting a character, fundamentally natural and probable with just one strange, wilful, wayward moral or physical deformity which upsets the equipoise and bears off the character from the world of tiresome reality and as far as the borderland of the fantastic.

Joyce's characters like Dickens's are "human-fantastic." From the first appearances of "Buck" Mulligan, Stephen, Haines, Deasy, Bloom, Molly, and Boylan, the reader knows that the people and the world of *Ulysses* are beyond "tiresome reality." The row of personages in the cameo-like portraits in Chapter X, "Wandering Rocks," is not only like a Dickensian row. Indeed, in keeping with warm *blood*, the part of the human body on which Joyce focuses in the chapter (as he tells us in the Linati and Gorman–Gilbert schemas),[5] the personages of "Wandering Rocks" include "warm-blooded" and fantastic literary "transfusions"—blendings, in fact, of Joyce's own characters and those of Dickens. The background of the chapter "The Hostile Environment," which Joyce said was its "meaning" in the Linati schema, also suggests the hostile city environment of many Dickens novels. A few examples from these cameo-like portraits and some comparisons with those in other chapters may help us to see how Joyce not only compares with Dickens in character portrayal, but how he alludes to him in his own creations.

Silk-hatted Father Conmee in Section I of Chapter X meets a one-legged sailor "growling" a song and extending his cap for alms. Conmee does not give him anything, but rather "blesses him in the sun." The one-legged balladeer suggests Silas Wegg, a one-legged vendor of fruit and ballads hobbling through the London streets in Dickens's *Our Mutual Friend*. In Chapter V Silas sings a patriotic ballad about his older brother, who parted from his beloved to enlist in the army. He sings it to support his claim to Boffin (who has employed him to read aloud the whole of *The Decline and Fall of the Roman Empire*) that he has been familiar since childhood with the "Decline-And-Fall-Off-The-Rooshan-Empire."[6] The one-legged sailor, as we learn in Section III, is singing the English patriotic song "The Death of Nelson" ("For England, home and beauty"). Conmee is not oblivious to the political overtones of the crippled sailor's song, but he is tight-fisted and indifferent toward this down-and-outer.

Weldon Thornton points out a direct character allusion to Dickens also in the first section of Chapter X:

> The repeated description of Maginni, who is a dancing master, in terms of "deportment" recalls the Turveydrops, father and son, from Charles Dickens' *Bleak House*. The son, Mr. Prince Turveydrop, is a dancing master and the elder Mr. Turveydrop is continually described as having "Deportment" (see esp. chap. XIV of the novel, entitled "Deportment").[7]

The human-fantastic characters with "deportment" in both novels are foils for the many characters whose bodies and souls are broken. There is an ironic twist also in that the characters with "deportment" are hollow men themselves. The disciplined steps of Maginni and Turveydrop Senior are mechanical and routine. They suggest the emptiness of the routines Father Conmee enacts at the beginning of the novel and those that the Viceroy and his retinue continue.

Another allusion to Dickens in the first section appears in the figure of Corny Kelleher, the assistant in H. J. O'Neill's funeral establishment, chewing a blade of hay, as Jerry Cruncher, the messenger and graverobber, chews straw and ruminates in Book II, Chapter I of *A Tale of Two Cities*. The ministers of the dead are also ministers of the living-dead in both novels, and foreshadow in their mastication of grass the natural decay of the body after death. Both nametags, "Corny" and "Cruncher," connote graveyards and corruption. That Corny also chews the blade of hay in Section II and in the "Hades" chapter suggests that the act is a mortality motif in the novel.

In Section III, the irony of the one-legged sailor singing "For England, home and beauty" as he passes Katey and Boody Dedalus is particularly apt since the anarchy of their father's "home" is not "beautiful." The brief incident leads into the picture in Section VI of Simon's poor and confused household which, as Harry Levin was first to point out in 1941, recalls that of Mr. Micawber in *David Copperfield*, except that there is no Mrs. Micawber there to try to hold it together. This lot falls on Maggy, who "at the range rammed down a greyish mass beneath bubbling suds twice with her potstick and wiped her brow" (226). The Dedalus children, like the sailor, depend on charity for their livelihood. The "yellow thick soup" that Maggy pours "from the kettle into a bowl" (226) and that Katey and Boody devour with bread, was given to them by Sister Mary Patrick at the nearby convent. Maggy, the drudge, seems to represent Eva Joyce, John Joyce's fourth daughter, who was twelve in June 1904.

Eva's brother Stanislaus Joyce, writing in his *Dublin Diary* under the entry for [29 February 1904], said: "My sister Eva reminds me of the 'Marchioness' in *The Old Curiosity Shop*."[8] Dickens's first descriptions of the Marchioness in Chapter XXXIV of that novel focus directly upon her as a drudging cook and housemaid in Samson Brass's house. Dick Swiveller "leaned over the table, and described a small slipshod girl in a dirty coarse apron and bib, which left nothing visible but her face and feet." This image of Dick leaning over the table and seeing the young girl was drawn by Frederick Barnard for an illustration that appears next to the description in the text. In the same entry in the *Diary* Stanislaus also connects a friend, "Miss Nolan," with a Dickens character and an illustration:

> The younger Miss Nolan wears her hair very tastefully in an old-fashioned style, parted in the centre and combed flat down. It is black and hangs in a plat behind. She is pretty and looks like as if she stepped out of a Cruikshank illustration to Dickens. I have nick-named her 'Dora.'[9]

Also, in the entry under the date [3 April 1904] Stanislaus says, "I call 7 S. Peter's Terrace, Cabra, 'Bleak House.' "[10] The address he mentions is where the Joyce family were living on June 4, 1904, and would correspond with Simon Dedalus's address and home in *Ulysses*, and the bleak picture of it in this section of "Wandering Rocks."

George Harris Healey, the editor of *The Complete Dublin Diary of Stanislaus Joyce*, says in his Preface that "James read these minutes while they were being written, asked to have them sent to him after he left Ireland, and borrowed from them the kind of small thing that none but James Joyce would have found worth borrowing at all."[11] Some "small things" that Joyce may have borrowed from Stanislaus's *Diary* are hints for cameos of Maggy at the stove in the kitchen steam and the bleak household. His recall would be directly from scenes at home that he himself had witnessed; but in this chapter, for which "resemblance" is a "symbol" in the Linati schema, he may also have had Stanislaus's notes in mind or recollections, in reference to Eva, of vignettes of the Marchioness from his reading of Dickens's novel. Joyce may have seen in three sentences of her first conversation with Dick Swiveller a sufficient Dickensian "resemblance" to Maggy: " 'Yes, I do plain cooking,' replied the child. 'I'm housemaid too; I do all the work of the house.' "

"Blazes" Boylan appears in Section V. He is brazen toward

the blond from whom he buys fruit for Molly. As a philandering theatrical man he may be compared with the philandering actor Jingle in *Pickwick*. The "jaunty jingle" that is a leitmotif for him plays on Jingle's "jaunty impudence," as Dickens describes it in Chapter II of *Pickwick*. T. S. Eliot has observed that "Dickens's figures belong to poetry, like figures of Dante or Shakespeare, in that a single phrase, either by them or about them, may be enough to set them wholly before us."[12] This insight may often be applied to Joyce's characters as well. It is not only true about Boylan's "jaunty jingle" but to the blond in this section, who "bestowed fat pears neatly, head by tail, and among them ripe shamefaced peaches" (227). When Boylan asks if the red carnation is for him, "The blond girl glanced sideways at him, got up regardless, with his tie a bit crooked, blushing" (228). She answers, yes. Then:

> Bending archly she reckoned again fat pears and blushing peaches.
> Blazes Boylan looked in her blouse with more favour, the stalk of the red flower between his smiling teeth. (228)

This poetic portrayal of the blond recalls Dickens's description of the youngest of the Five Sisters of York in *Nicholas Nickleby*, Chapter VI: "The blushing tints in the soft bloom on the fruit, or the delicate painting on the flower, are not more exquisite than was the blending of the rose and lily in her gentle face, or the deep blue of her eye."

A key to Section VI is sentiment. Almidano Artifoni, Stephen's music teacher, is a sympathetic man. His gaze "over Stephen's shoulder at Goldsmith's knobby poll" (the *head* of his statue near Trinity College) is significant. In his concern for Stephen's musical career Artifoni is a sentimentalist like Goldsmith, to reiterate an analogy from Joyce's essay on Dickens.

Joyce took the name Almidano Artifoni from that of the director of the Berlitz School in Trieste, for whom he taught; but the character is in the main based on Father Charles Ghezzi, Joyce's Italian teacher at the University, who, as Ellmann says, "appears in Joyce's books with a benign character and the euphonious name of Almidano Artifoni."[13]

Almidano's Italian and his gestures express *gentilezza:* "His heavy hand took Stephen's firmly. Human eyes. They gazed curiously an instant and turned quickly towards a Dalkey tram" (228). As he "trotted" in vain to catch the tram, he recalls "Trotty" Veck in Dickens's *The Chimes:* "A weak, small, spare old man, he was a very Hercules, this Toby, in his good intentions." The music of the Chimes relates to Artifoni, the music teacher. When Almidano says *"il mondo è una bestia"* (228), he refers to the hostile environment which is also very much evident in the Malthusian characters surrounding "Trotty." Artifoni's serious concern for music and Stephen is set off in this section by students' stealing "implements of music" from the university library, and, as he walks on in Section XVII, by mad Cashel Boyle O'Connor Fitzmaurice Tisdall Farrell's roughly brushing up against the blind piano tuner. Joyce's views that Dickens was a great caricaturist like Hogarth and a great sentimentalist like Goldsmith are combined and come into focus in his portrayal of Almidano.

Two more Dickensian similarities warrant attention at this point. In Section IX the haughty "lawyers of the past" suggest the self-serving lawyers who prolong the Jarndyce lawsuit for nearly a hundred years in *Bleak House.* And the chancery court injustices suffered by the elderly, black-clad Miss Flite in the same novel are somewhat reflected in the frustrations of the elderly female with a black skirt who rustles from the King's Bench to the Court of Appeal in this section of *Ulysses.* As we learn in Section X she has heard cases in the Lord Chancellor's court, in the Admiralty division, and in the Court of Appeals. Is her plight similar to Miss Flite's? Does she, like Miss Flite, attend multitudes of hearings in expectation of her own case coming up, and in fear of missing it? The modern world, like the law courts that are metaphors for the quality of that world, are plagued by Wiglomerations, endless and hopeless comings and goings, for both the old ladies.

In Section XIII the two old women, one with an umbrella and one with a midwife's bag, also resemble the midwife Sarah Gamp, who carries an umbrella and a midwife's bag, and her coworker, Betsey Prigg, in *Martin Chuzzlewit.* These women appeared first at the beginning of the "Proteus" chapter. Weldon Thornton analyzes the sentence, "Number one swung lourdily her midwife's bag, the other's gamp poked in the beach," as follows:

> In light of the proximate mention of a "midwife's bag," it is likely that Stephen uses *gamp* because of Mrs. Gamp, the umbrella-carrying monthly nurse in Dickens' *Martin Chuzzlewit.* Dickens tells us that Mrs. Gamp's sign-board proclaimed her "Midwife," and that at her first appearance in the novel she has just been up all night helping another "professional lady" deliver a child (chap. 19). This character's name is the source of the word *gamp* to mean *umbrella.* That Mrs. Gamp had an imaginary friend named Mrs. Harris makes the allusion more appropriate to this Protean chapter.[14]

It may be added that it is also appropriate to illusionary as well as allusionary "resemblances" of "Wandering Rocks."

I think we can see from the brief glance at several characters in Chapter X that Joyce fixes people memorably in our minds because we see them "in the light of one strongly-marked or even exaggerated moral or physical quality." An illustrator such as "Phiz" (the pseudonym of Hablôt K. Browne) or George

Cruikshank would easily have been able to depict Joyce's caricatures in drawings. Some aspects of Joyce's characters may,
moreover, be seen in illustrations to Dickens. Of the Dickens's
characters I have mentioned, Silas Wegg, Turveydrop, Jerry
Cruncher, the Marchioness, Jingle, "Trotty" Veck, Miss Flite, and
Sarah Gamp have been portrayed by Dickens's illustrators. The
recurring image of "A charming *soubrette,* great Marie Kendall,
with dauby cheeks and lifted skirt" smiling "daubily from her
poster" (253) suggests that Joyce had caricature-type illustrations in mind for the poses and actions of his characters in this
chapter. We should not forget, however, that Joyce went beyond
caricature in his character portrayal.

Though similarities to Dickens help us recognize the
Hogarthian qualities in Joyce's characters, as well as point up
his method as a "city" novelist, they also work in other ways;
they are often symbolic of life in Giambattista Vico's democratic,
or Human, Age. Joyce's overall vision in *Ulysses* is largely based
on Vico's Three Ages of Man: the Divine, the Heroic, the
Human, and a *ricorso,* or cyclical recommencement of the three
Ages. Vico explains his three Ages in *The New Science* (1725),
the major forerunner of modern cyclical studies of history. Its
newness derived from Vico's idea that man knows what he himself creates. Consciousness alone is not knowledge. Man can be
conscious of nature, but he cannot know it as God does. Man
has, however, created his world and history; and he can come to
know it. Vico tries to unveil the causes underlying civilization
and history that previously were thought to be locked in God's
mind or to be only indirectly accessible through revelation or
myth, or in the acts of extraordinary heroes. Vico's thought is
empirical and philological. It is, perhaps, the first philosophy of
history.

Vico discusses twelve major characteristics of the Three

Ages in *The New Science*. I shall mention a few. Humanity in the Divine Age is childlike and poetic and deifies all that surrounds it, thunder and lightning most of all; in the Heroic Age, sacred marriage, pride in family, and force are dominant; in the Human Age reason prevails, and laws, industry, commerce, art, and science with it. Malicious use of reason tended to vitiate the Human Age, and monarchy, or a cyclical return, or *ricorso*, to religious values tended to follow. Ellmann in *Ulysses on the Liffey* says:

> Joyce followed Vico but at his own pace; he held, as Vico did not, that the best political system was the democratic one. But he embraced eagerly Vico's cycle of three ages, theocratic, aristocratic, and democratic, concluding in a *ricorso* and another cycle. The *ricorso* was not so much a turnabout, as promotion from experience to experience comprehended and known. Joyce said in a letter that the theory had amply demonstrated itself in his life, and quite possibly he saw himself as having begun in fear of God, then basking in family and personal pride, and finally, dispossessed, discovering a sufficient value in the ordinary and unassuming. That, at any rate, is the grace shadowed in *Ulysses*.[15]

In his admiration for Vico and yet a preference for democracy, Joyce is akin to Jules Michelet, one of the strongest nineteenth-century Viconian liberals and a major influence on Joyce's later work. Though Michelet admits that Vico's thought pervades his work, he does not agree with Vico's view that monarchy is the best form of government. Michelet as characterized by William Dismukes,

> gives Vico's idea that man is his own Prometheus a fresh interpretation and shows history to be a progressive triumph of liberty over fatality, of mind over matter. Like Vico, Michelet is a social historian seeking to animate the anonymous masses who

have created history and for whom the heroes have only been the spokesmen.

He adds:

> An apparent departure from the principles of Vico in the *Histoire de France* is noticed in the condemnation of monarchy, the form of government which seemed most satisfactory to Vico. Michelet is an advocate of democracy and takes every opportunity to denounce the evils of monarchical government.[16]

Joyce often refers to Michelet in *Finnegans Wake* and quotes, translates, or parodies a sentence from Edgar Quinet, Michelet's Viconian friend, many times in the *Wake*. Joyce's adapting Vico's ideas into *Ulysses* and the *Wake* is in the liberal spirit of both Michelet and Quinet.

How does Joyce's Paduan essay on Dickens relate to Vico's cycles in *Ulysses?* His view that Dickens has been rightly called "the great Cockney" marks him not only as a creator of city life and characters, but as the spirited upstart democrat whose outlook on life was consistent with typical liberal views on Vico such as Michelet's and Quinet's. Dickens from his earliest years as a writer was a liberal (in the Leigh Hunt and Victor Hugo traditions) who was aware of class and cultural conflicts, and who cultivated a natural sensitivity to historical issues. Dickens may have been aware of Vico's ideas since they were very much in the air in the nineteenth century. Coleridge from 1816 had been reading and touting Vico in London.[17] Other intellectuals admired Vico's ideas and books, and may have impressed on Dickens his importance in the liberal cause or possibly in the broad church movement.[18] Floris Delattre in *Dickens et la France* sees an affinity between Dickens's liberal and humanist views and those of Michelet and Quinet.[19] Michelet's book on Vico, published in 1827 and reissued in 1835 under the title *Oeuvres*

Choisie de Vico, impressed some critics as a better exposition of the Italian thinker's views than his own.[20] A curious fact is that Dickens met Michelet and Quinet in Paris in 1844 and they talked about Guizot,[21] another historian who was interested in Vico and whom Dickens had met in 1840. Since Michelet began his *History of France* (1833–1867) with Vico's idea that man creates his own history,[22] (an idea which strengthened the liberal stance in the nineteenth century) Dickens, who in 1844 was a forceful liberal in England, would probably enjoy talking to him about political issues in which Vico played a prominent part.

Whether Joyce suspected that there were affinities between Dickens and Michelet and Quinet or between Dickens and Vico in his awareness of Dickens's liberal attitudes or in specific areas of his writing, is an open question. But, besides the tenor of the similarities with Dickens in *Ulysses* and *Finnegans Wake* that evoke Dickens's sympathetic responses to the common man and protest against social evils, there is some evidence that Joyce did envision Dickens from the point of view of Vico's system in one of his *Finnegans Wake Workbooks* (circa 1923).

A few pages after he mentions Michelet and Quinet, Joyce jotted down the highly charged phrases "Dean Hercules Dickens on/the wet root (spud)/G. Petrie M. Jerome/(no epitaph)/R. Emmet/Thee was in him/De Danaan Gods seek/aid of heroes in fights."[23] These breaks in phrasings are Joyce's. Madame Raphael, Joyce's amanuensis, copied over the dog-eared, torn-paged, and obviously much-used holograph notebook. Madame Raphael's transcription of these words is the same as Joyce's in the original notebook. No words in the above quotation are crossed out with colored pencil in the holograph or the transcription, which was Joyce's usual way of signifying that they were used in the *Wake*.

Focusing on "Dean Hercules Dickens on/the wet root (spud)," we can see that each of the first three words suggest one of Vico's three Ages of Man, and the "wet root (spud)" is possibly a *ricorso*. *Dean* could signify the Irish Danaan gods or any ecclesiastical dean (perhaps Dean Swift) and hence would refer to the Divine Age. *Hercules*, like Ulysses, would signify the Heroic Age. *Dickens* is in the third, human or democratic, position.

I have found in reading the *Wake* that similarities to Dickens found in that work seem to connote the Human or Democratic Age, or perhaps the other two ages or *ricorsos* seen from a Dickensian vista. In I, vi, the Viconian tenor of "Dean Hercules Dickens" seems to be implicit in Nuvoletta's reaction to the Mookse and the Gripes, who, arguing heatedly, do not notice her or her winsome double Nuvoluccia:

> Not even her feignt reflection, Nuvoluccia, could they toke their gnoses off for their minds with intrepfide fate and bungless curiasity, were conclaved with Heliogobbleus and Commodus and Enobarbarus and whatever the coordinal dickens they did as their damprauch of papyrs and buchstubs said. As if that was their spiration! (157)

Humphrey or HCE, the protagonist of *Finnegans Wake*, is implicit in *H*eliogobbleus, Commodus, and Enobarbarus. Heliogobbleus suggests Heliogabalus, a Roman emperor who enforced the worship of a sun-god, hence a theocratic age in Roman history. Commodus was a weak Roman emperor who might signify a shaky aristocratic or heroic age. Enobarbarus suggests Mark Antony's traitorous friend Enobarbus in Shakespeare's *Antony and Cleopatra* and the most malicious, or most barbarous aspects of plebeian lack of honor in the democratic age, especially in comparison with heroic Antony. The names, Nuvoletta and Nuvoluccia, suggest renewal or Viconian rebirth or *ricorso*. Nuvoletta is dismayed at the Mookse and the Gripes's debating Roman history and not seeing her as their "spiration," their spiraling aspiration. The evoking of "coordinal dickens" counters the intellectual argument with a sense of rebirth into feelings from the heart in democratic spiritual equality. Latent in the word "coordinal" are puns that hint at Dickens being a "cardinal" or hinge of the new age which would be based on equality ("coordinal" rather than "super-ordinal") and heartfelt (from the "bosom's inmost core") or cordial feelings ("coordinal" as a pun on the Latin word for heart, cor, cordis).

Another sentimental allusion to Dickens relevant to Vico in *Finnegans Wake* may be seen in the following quotation from I, vi:

> speared the rod and spoiled the lightning; married with cakes and repunked with pleasure; till he was buried howhappy was he and he made the welkins ring with *"Up Micawber!"* (131)

Here the focus is on the awe of lightning prevalent in Vico, an awe that made primitive man turn to religion and would eventually result in the Divine Age; marriage, a mark of the Heroic Age; burial, associated with the Human Age in Vico's system; and rebirth via Wilkins Micawber in *David Copperfield*, in whom "hope springs eternal in the human heart."

Joyce's point in the Padua essay that Dickens was a sentimentalist like Goldsmith also suggests that connections with Dickens in *Ulysses* might gravitate around sentimental and sympathetic themes. We know this is the case in the stylistic Dickensian echoes and an allusion to "Doady" in *David Copperfield* in Joyce's depiction of Mina Purefoy and her newborn babe, in Chapter XIV, "The Oxen of the Sun":

> And as her loving eyes behold her babe she wishes only one blessing more, to have her dear Doady there with her to share her joy, to lay in his arms that mite of God's clay, the fruit of

their lawful embraces. He is older now (you and I may whisper it) and a trifle stooped in the shoulders yet in the whirligig of years a grave dignity has come to the conscientious second accountant of the Ulster bank, College Green branch. (420–21)

The position of this passage appears in the evolution of literature progression (the linguistic and literary equivalent of "ontogeny recapitulates phylogeny"). It is in a democratic phase of a succession of passages that have earlier expressed theocratic and aristocratic phases. Dickens's sentiment in its best sense is deeply shared love; it is a form of popular sympathetic wisdom similar to that which prevails in the best moments of Vico's democratic Age.

Joyce wished to present the *Ulysses* myth *sub specie temporis nostris* in *Ulysses*. The "mirror of our times" reflects everyday Dublin life on June 16, 1904.[24] But because Dickens's fiction was so close in time and place to Joyce's, echoes of his works in *Ulysses* offer some poetic perspectives on "our times." The reader may hold the mirror a little further away from that one day in Dublin and see some Dickensian reflections that add representative significance to Joyce's Dubliners in Vico's Human or "democratic" Age. At a further distance the mirror would reflect the Ulysses myth and the Heroic Age; at even a further distance, the Bible and the Divine Age. Reflections of the Human Age in the mirror of our times are not exclusively Dickensian, but then again those of the other two Ages are not exclusively Homeric or biblical.

Joyce's writing "Dean Hercules Dickens" in 1923, a year after the publication of *Ulysses,* may be retrospective, as well as forward-looking to *Finnegans Wake,* even as many other entries in the *Wake Workbooks* incorporate retrospective references to, or notes on, *Ulysses.* Bearing in mind thoughts from Joyce's essay on Dickens, from connections that other critics and scholars have noted, and some critical inferences that may be drawn retrospectively from the note in his *Workbook* and its connection with the passages in *Finnegans Wake*, there seem to be many areas for extended studies of correspondences between Dickens and Joyce.

Ellmann in *Ulysses on the Liffey* interprets the Viconian structuring of *Ulysses* in a progressive sequence. In his view, Chapter I is primarily theocratic; its language is sacred and its wisdom, oracular. Chapter II is primarily aristocratic; its language, symbolic and its wisdom, devious; Chapter III is primarily democratic; its language, the vernacular and its wisdom, sympathetic. Each succeeding group of three chapters mainly follow this pattern.[25] R. M. Adams agrees with Ellmann,[26] but thinks that each democratic chapter contains a *ricorso*, or rebirth. I should like to suggest that the symbolic references to Vico's three Ages are also *tiered* in character-portrayals in each chapter, as well as being extended through progressive triads of chapters, and that there are frequently correspondences with Dickens's democratic Age or *ricorso* or in other Ages as seen from the perspective of the democratic Age or that of a *ricorso*.

Because allusions to Dickens appear in each chapter of *Ulysses*, only a book-length study of them and their correspondences to Vico's views can encompass fully their significance. What follows is one among many examples, however, that seem to substantiate the points that have been made here. In Chapter VI, "Hades," a democratic chapter in Ellmann's schema,[27] Martin Cunningham is introduced to us as a generally good Christian; he organizes Paddy Dignam's funeral and starts the collection to pay for young Dignam's education. Father Conmee later in the novel refers to him as a "good practical Catholic" (219). He is religious and expresses *largesse de coeur* in a chapter for which Joyce in his Linati schema has indicated "The Sacred Heart" as a symbol.[28] In Chapter XII, "Cyclops," he helps Bloom escape from the raging citizen. On the religious Viconian plane he is clearly a good samaritan. On the heroic plane, as Joyce notes in "correspondences" in the Gorman plan,[29] he is a surrogate for Sisyphus, whose punishment in Hades is to push a huge rock to the top of a mountain; and after it rolled back down, to push it up again, *ad nauseam*. On the human, or democratic, plane, there seems to be a direct literary analogue between Cunningham and Stephen Blackpool in Dickens's *Hard Times*. Both Cunningham and Blackpool have alcoholic wives whom they are barely able to support because they pawn the household furniture to buy liquor and live loosely.

Bloom looks at Cunningham and thinks: "Sympathetic human man he is. Intelligent. Like Shakespeare's face. Always a good word to say" (96). Further thoughts that come to Bloom about Cunningham seem to be textual allusions to *Hard Times*. Bloom thinks:

And that awful drunkard of a wife of his. Setting up house for her time after time and then pawning the furniture on him every Saturday almost. Leading him the life of the damned. Wear the heart out of a stone, that. Monday morning start afresh. Shoulder to the wheel. Lord, she must have looked a sight that night, Dedalus told me he was in there. Drunk about the place and capering with Martin's umbrella:

> *And they call me the jewel of Asia,*
> *Of Asia,*
> *The geisha. (96)*

Blackpool talks about his wife to Bounderby in Book I, Chapter XI, as follows:

I were married on Eas'r Mondy nineteen years sin, long and dree. She were a young lass—pretty enow—wi' good accounts of herseln. Well! She went bad—soon. Not along of me. Gonnows I were not a unkind husband to her.

Bounderby replies:

> I have heard all this before. . . . She took to drinking, left off
> working, sold the furniture, pawned the clothes, and played old
> Gooseberry.

To play "old Gooseberry" is to play the deuce or the devil, which
is what Mrs. Cunningham does when she is drunk. Blackpool is
characterized throughout *Hard Times* as a kind, reasonable and
suffering man as is Cunningham. He tells Bounderby that he
has tried to be patient with his wife, but like Mrs. Cunningham
she sold or pawned everything over and over again:

> I ha' gone home, many's the time, and found all vanished as I
> had in the world, and her without a sense left to bless herseln
> lying on the bare ground. I ha' dun't not once, not twice—
> twenty time!

She then went from bad to worse. She "disgraced herseln every-
ways" and then returned and repeated the pattern. The pictures
that Dickens and Joyce paint of alcoholic wives are similar to
Hogarth's picture of an inebriated woman near a pawnshop in
his etching "Gin Alley." Is it a coincidence? Perhaps, but the
couples still may be relevant to Vico's democratic epoch. The
wives in this case do exemplify the worst "spirits" and the hus-
bands the best "spirits" of Vico's all too Human Age.

Some deeper meanings seem to emerge from relating the
Dubliner Cunningham to Blackpool, whose name is the literal
translation of the word *Dublin* from Gaelic into English. *Dubh*
meaning *black* and *linn* meaning *pool* is the etymology of
Dublin. Dublin was named originally for the village that sprang
up at the confluence of the Liffey and Poddle rivers. The water
was black because the bottom of Dublin harbor was so deep

that it could not be seen from the surface.[30] Blackpool's name connotes the "blackpool" of the hardships he endures in "black" Coketown in *Hard Times*. It also connotes the "hellish" black mine pit into which he falls and dies and, by extension, death itself, which is the motif of the "Hades" chapter of *Ulysses* wherein Cunningham is first fully introduced to us in the novel and figures as the hell-death sufferer Sisyphus, whom Ulysses-Bloom encounters on his journey to the Hades cemetery.

That Joyce consciously had *Hard Times* and other Dickens novels in mind in writing *Ulysses* is borne out in Chapter XVI, "Eumaeus," the style of which is "old narrative." That chapter is sprinkled with titles of "old" novels. There, Gumley, the sentryman asleep in his sentry box, is depicted as having fallen from his earlier job that paid a hundred pounds a year into a "truly amazing piece of hard times" (639). This would seem to be a direct allusion to Dickens's *Hard Times*, since Gumley is also described as being at "the end of his tether," a phrase that suggests the title of Conrad's story "The End of the Tether." The *Hard Times* allusion in the context of other references to Dickens's novels in this episode[31] does seem to bolster the point that Joyce is directly alluding to Dickens in the novel.

The connections between Cunningham and Blackpool are close, but there is also coincidence in the similarities between Cunningham and the life of Matthew Kane, the Dubliner who was most likely a source for the character of Cunningham. Stanislaus Joyce tells us in *My Brother's Keeper* that Matthew Kane had a dipsomaniac wife who pawned furniture to buy drink and who was institutionalized for alcoholism.[32] Granted that Joyce based the character of Cunningham on correspondences with Kane's life, his fictive genius expanded them to include qualities of Cunningham's inner life, his sensitivity, for example, to thoughts of suicide similar to those of Blackpool, along with the other details about Blackpool that we can so closely correlate with Cunningham's situation. Joyce, as a symbolist artist, would welcome correspondences with figures and events from Dickens to extend the biographical references and make them more universally representative of Vico's democratic age.

Notes

AFTERWORD II

[1] James Joyce, *Ulysses* (New York: Random House, 1961), p. 57. Further references to *Ulysses* will be to this edition with page numbers in parentheses.

[2] Frank Budgen, *James Joyce and the Making of Ulysses*, with an Introduction by Hugh Kenner (Bloomington and London: Indiana University Press, 1967), p. 72.

[3] G. K. Chesterton, *Charles Dickens: A Critical Study* (New York: Dodd, Mead and Co., 1911).

[4] James Joyce, "Drama and Life," *Critical Writings, op. cit.*, p. 40.

[5] See Ellmann, *Ulysses on the Liffey* (New York: Oxford University Press, 1972), p. 188, and Stuart Gilbert, *James Joyce's ULYSSES* (New York: Knopf, 1930), p. 208.

[6] Quotations from and references to Dickens will be to the New Century Edition (Boston: Dana Estes and Co., 1900) and will be indicated by chapter numbers. The reader refrains from calling Father Conmee a "Scrooge" but Joyce suggests the connection: "He thought, but not for long, of soldiers and sailors, whose legs had been shot off by cannonballs, ending their days in some pauper ward" (219). When Scrooge is asked for a contribution for the needy, he answers that there are "establishments" for them. Joyce also suggests the connection in Chapter XV, "Circe," which Harry Levin has described as a Dantean and Scrooge-like dream. Conmee and the sailor appear there in reversed circumstances: "*Conmee on Christass lame crutch and leg sailor in cockboat armfolded . . .*" (579). This passage appears in "The Dance of Death," where, as in Dante's *Inferno*, punishments are commensurate with sins, the first are last, the maltreaters are repaid with maladies appropriate to them. Conmee's appearing on a "Christass lame crutch" suggests, besides the "leg sailor," Tiny Tim's lameness and crutch in Dickens's *A Christmas Carol*, and a fitting punishment for an unrepentant, tight-fisted

Scrooge. If the phrase were "Christmass" rather than "Christass lame crutch" the correspondence with Tiny Tim would probably be more conclusive. But as it reads, Conmee, suffering as a cripple in the fantasy, evokes the humility that he lacks. He may even learn from that condition what Tiny Tim thinks about himself as a Christian *exemplum*. Tiny Tim told his father coming home from church, "that he hoped the people saw him in the church, because he was a cripple, and it might be pleasant to them to remember upon Christmas Day who made lame beggars walk and blind men see." Conme, going about institutional business in Chapter X, does not remember who made lame beggars walk and blind men see, even though he "sees" the lame sailor directly before him. Conmee is one of Joyce's best-drawn characters. He is not morose and unsociable as Scrooge is, but there is a soupçon of the old skinflint and pauper-warder in him that calls Scrooge (before his conversion) to mind.

[7] Weldon Thornton, *Allusions in ULYSSES* (Chapel Hill: University of North Carolina Press, 1968), p. 222.

[8] Stanislaus Joyce, *The Complete Dublin Diary of Stanislaus Joyce*, ed. and with a Preface by George H. Healey (Ithaca and London: Cornell University Press, 1971), p. 14.

[9] *Ibid.*, p. 13.

[10] *Ibid.*, p. 39.

[11] George H. Healey, Preface, *op. cit.*, p. vii.

[12] T. S. Eliot, "Wilkie Collins and Dickens" in *Selected Essays* (New York: Harcourt Brace, 1950), p. 411.

[13] Ellmann, *James Joyce, op. cit.*, p. 61.

[14] *Allusions in ULYSSES, op. cit.*, pp. 43–44.

[15] *Ulysses on the Liffey*, p. 52.

[16] William Paul Dismukes, "Michelet and Vico: A Study of Michelet's Use of Vichian Principles," An Abstract of a Doctoral Thesis at the University of Illinois (Urbana, Illinois, 1936), p. 10.

[17] See Max Harold Fisch and Thomas Goddard Bergin, Introduction to the *Autobiography of Giambattista Vico*, trans. by Fisch and Bergin (Ithaca, New York: Great Seal Books, A Division of Cornell University Press, 1963), pp. 83–89.

[18] Fisch and Bergin, *op. cit.*, pp. 61–107, indicate that a large number of more or less prominent thinkers in Europe, England and Ireland, and the United States, before and during Dickens's time, knew or used Vico's ideas. Among the Italian figures they mention

is Giuseppe Mazzini: "If Vico's reputation had hitherto been predominantly Neapolitan, it now became Italian and international; and the *New Science* became the book of the Risorgimento. Wherever Italian patriots went—Foscolo, Prati and Mazzini to England, Ferrari and Gioberti to France and Belgium—they carried it in hand or in mind . . . Ferrari edited his works (1835–37) and made 'Vico and Italy' a war cry of nationalism. Prati lent the *New Science* to Coleridge at Highgate. Mazzini wrote Ugoni from London in 1839 that if Ferrari's edition were at hand he would attempt an article in *The British and Foreign Review* on the doctrines of Vico, 'unknown or misunderstood here' " (p. 66). Dickens met Mazzini with the Carlyles in 1844 and championed his liberal movement to free and unify Italy, helped him to raise funds, and protested against government censorship of his mail. See Una Pope-Hennessey, *Charles Dickens* (New York: Howell, Soskin, Pubs., Inc., 1946), pp. 208–9. Also see Forster's *Life of Dickens* and Edgar Johnson's biography *Charles Dickens, op. cit.,* and *Dickens' Letters* (London: Nonesuch Press, 1938) for further connections between Dickens and Mazzini. Among French thinkers influenced by Vico whom Fisch and Bergin mention, Dickens had personally met Guizot, Michelet, and Quinet. Dickens may have known about or read Michelet's *Oeuvres Choisies de Vico*, first published in 1827 and re-issued in 1835. Among English rationalist Viconians close to Dickens, there was John Stuart Mill (who wrote for the liberal editor of the *Morning Chronicle,* John Black, when Dickens also wrote for the *Chronicle* in 1834). Fisch and Bergin mention that Mill referred to Vico's theory of cycles in his *System of Logic* of 1834, but add that he probably drew from Michelet. Thomas Arnold was a Broad Church Movement thinker whom Dickens admired. Fisch and Bergin point out that Arnold was the first English historian to admit to Vico's influence.

[19] Floris Delattre, *Dickens et la France: ETUDE D'UNE INTER-ACTION LITTERAIRE ANGLO-FRANÇAISE* (Paris: Librairie Universitaire, J. Gambier, Editeur, 1927). Delattre's first two sentences in this book connect Dickens with Victor Hugo, Alfred de Vigny, and Michelet and Quinet. In Section III, "Le Roman de Dickens et le naturalisme Français," Delattre draws a close parallel between Dickens and Michelet and Quinet in the tradition of French romanticism and liberalism. Floris Delattre's essay "Le Centenaire de Charles Dickens," which first appeared in *La Revue Pedagogique*

(January 1912) and then in *De Byron à Francis Thompson* (Paris: Librairie Payot, 1913), contains some striking parallels with Joyce's "The Centenary of Charles Dickens." Besides discussing caricature and sentiment, the way in which Dickens evokes city smells, his minute realistic descriptions and unique characters touched by reality, fantasy, and exaggeration, and his popular appeal—all items that Joyce talks about in his Dickens essay—Delattre uses two expressions that might have appealed to Joyce if he read the essay and that do pertain to *Ulysses*. One is the expression "la joie sérieuse" which connects in *Ulysses* with the word *jocoserious* (677); the other is *dédale* (which means labyrinth or confusion). The word *dédale* is used in *Ulysses* (423).

[20] See Fisch and Bergin's comments and their quotation of Robert Flint's view in 1884, *op. cit.*, p. 77.

[21] See Edgar Johnson, *Charles Dickens: His Tragedy and Triumph* (New York: Simon and Shuster, 1952), Vol. I, p. 537. François Guizot (1787–1874) was a French historian who as early as 1817 expressed interest in Vico. See Fisch and Bergin, *op. cit.*, pp. 74–75: "Guizot, soliciting an article for the *Archives philosophiques* in 1817, wrote Furiel: 'If you have time to do one on Vico too, that would be splendid.'" Dickens had met Guizot at a party at Buller's in 1840 where and when he also met Carlyle. See Johnson, *op. cit.*, Vol. I, p. 316.

[22] See Fisch and Bergin, *op. cit.*, p. 79, on Michelet: "The introduction to universal history was composed at top speed after the revolution of July, 1830; dashed off he later said, 'on the burning pavements of Paris.' It opened with these words: 'With the world began a war which will end only with the world: the war of man against nature, of spirit against matter, of liberty against fatality. History is nothing other than the record of this interminable struggle.' This view of history as a struggle of liberty against fatality, which Michelet identified with Vico's conception of man making his own history, became the dominant theme of his great history of France, which was inspired by the same July revolution but was forty years in the writing. Looking back on his labors in his preface of 1869, Michelet wrote: 'I had no master but Vico. His principle of living force, of humanity creating itself, made both my book and my teaching.'"

[23] MS. Buffalo, VI.B.2.: "*Finnegans Wake*: Holograph of Work-

books" in *James Joyce's Manuscripts and Letters at the University of Buffalo: A Catalogue*, compiled and with an Introduction by Peter Spielberg (Buffalo: Buffalo University, 1962), pp. 129–30. For transcription see MS. VI.C.2.

[24] *Letters*, I, pp. 146–47.

[25] *Ulysses on the Liffey*, see pp. 58–59, pp. 118–24, 178–83.

[26] R. M. Adams, "Hades," in *James Joyce's Ulysses: Critical Essays*, ed. by Clive Hart and David Hayman (Berkeley, Los Angeles, London: University of California Press, 1974), p. 114.

[27] See Ellmann, *Ulysses on the Liffey*, p. 59.

[28] *Ibid.*, p. 188.

[29] *Idem.*

[30] See Brendan O Hehir, *A Gaelic Lexicon for FINNEGANS WAKE and Glossary for Joyce's Other Works* (Berkeley and Los Angeles: University of California Press, 1967), p. 381. The origin of *Dublin* has also been connected with the black peat bogs that could be seen at the bottom of the clear water.

[31] Joyce seems to allude to *Great Expectations* (651); *Pickwick Papers* (621); and *The Old Curiosity Shop* (621), as well as *Our Mutual Friend* (635).

[32] Stanislaus Joyce in *My Brother's Keeper: James Joyce's Early Years*, ed. with Intro. and Notes by Richard Ellmann and with a Preface by T. S. Eliot (New York: Viking Press, 1958), pp. 225–26. "He had a good position as chief clerk in the solicitor general's office, but was burdened with a wife who was an incorrigible drunkard. He had set up house for her two or three times during her periods of reformation, but she sold the furniture and neglected her young children, so that at the time I speak of he had put his wife in a home for inebriates and his children in a school."

NOTES
on the
THESIS-READER'S
CORRECTIONS

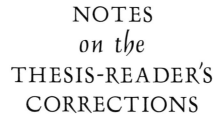

Note: The numbers given for "paragraph" and "line" refer to the holograph of Joyce's Renaissance essay, not to the printed version.

PARAGRAPH LINE

1   1   La dottrina evoluzionista, nella luce della quale la nostra società si bea, c'insegna che quando eravamo piccoli non eravamo ancora grandi: *Evoluzionistica* is the proper word and spelling. The vertical squiggle in the left margin seems to say that the reader did not appreciate Joyce's irony against the fatuous or truistic application of the evolutionary theory to history.

1   9   il nome di adulto: *adulto,* used here as a noun, is acceptable Italian. The "English Schoolmistress" seems to have been persnickety in this correction.

1   9–10   E una conclusione molto drastica . . . : *drastica* is acceptable, though the word is not as commonly used in Italian as "drastic" is in English.

1   12   Il progresso tanto strombazzato di questo secolo consiste in gran parte in un groviglio di macchine il cui scopo è appunto quello di raccogliere in fretta e furia gli elementi sparpagliati dell'utile e dello scibile e di ridistribuirli ad ogni membro della collettività che sia in grado di pagare una tenue tassa: This may have been questioned as a rambling sentence. Internal punctuations to separate parenthetical expressions might have helped.

1   22   strada di una grande città moderna: il tram elettrico il fili telegrafici . . . aziende commerciali ecc.: This sentence seems to be free from any technical errors. A very literal reader may find that it strays in its examples from the mechanical conquests and discoveries that it set out to illustrate.

PARAGRAPH   LINE

1   26   la mente umana terrorizzata quasi dalla grandezza materiale si perde . . . : *terrorizzata* is the past participle of *terrorizzare* and is acceptable, though the word might have been considered a Gallicism (and neologism) in 1912. A linguistic purist might have been inclined to frown on the expression at that time.

1   28   la mente . . . rinnega se stessa e s'infrollisce . . . : Joyce's diction may be in question here. *La mente . . . s'indebolisce* might be more acceptable. It is, however, less metaphorical and colorful than s'infrollisce.

1   31   atrofizza le facoltà spirituali dell'uomo . . . : *atrofizza*, derived from the transitive verb, *atrofizzare*, "to atrophy," is acceptable Italian though the figure of speech is quite bold and striking.

1   32   ne smussa la finezza . . . : *smussa*, derived from the transitive verb *smussare*, "to blunt," is acceptable; the word, however, also means "to smoothen," or "to round out rough edges," in a sense, the opposite of "to blunt"; and we can understand the reader's underlining it.

2   9   non era perche il sistema : *perche* should be *perchè* with the accent mark.

2   10   non era perche il sistema in se stesso gli era alieno. : This should be gli *fosse* alieno.

2   11   E cosi quando i grandi ribelli . . . abbracciò il nuovo vangelo: This long sentence might benefit from commas and parentheses; but, as most long and complex sentences, it might still be hard to follow. *cosi* also takes the accent mark, *così*.

2   19   udì la voce del mondo visuale . . . : *visibile* would probably be a word more commonly used in this context than *visuale* which might still be acceptable.

Notes on the Thesis-Reader's Corrections

PARAGRAPH	LINE	
2	20	ove si vive e si muore, si pecca e si pente . . . : *si pente* seems to be correct and acceptable.
2	24	come Dio stanco (mi si passi la parola alquanto irriverente) delle sue perfezioni divine chiama il creato fuori del . . . : This seemingly complex idea that Joyce bases on Bruno's theory of contraries could very well have seemed obscure or extravagant to the reader.
2	32	senza il quale non può realizzarsi . . . : *realizzarsi* means "to come true" as well as to "realize itself" or "to come into being." The ambiguity may have been disconcerting.
2	39	?(o almeno per giudicare): *valutare*, "to evaluate," would be more appropriate Italian diction than *giudicare*, "to judge."
3	3	che l'ondata del rinascimento portò alle nuvole (o gùi di li) . . . : *li* should read *lì* with the accent mark.
3	6	? e terminare con la preghiera rituale . . . : The reader might be bewildered here by Joyce's appropriating an expression from religion as a metaphor for the appreciation of Renaissance figures. The expression, perhaps less frequently used in Italian than "ritual prayer" in English, is nonetheless acceptable.
3	13	?ha messo il giornalista nella cattedra del monaco . . . : *giornalista* is acceptable Italian for "journalist." *Corrispondente* would perhaps be a more formal word and less likely to be a neologism and questionable. The antithesis between the journalist and the monk is so original and striking that we can understand how a reader might be troubled by it. The best reaction would simply be to appreciate the insight it fosters.
3	20	Shakespeare e Lope de Vega sono responsabili, fino ?ad un certo punto, per il cinematografo: the preposi-

JAMES JOYCE IN PADUA

tion *di* normally follows *responsabile. Per il* should read *del.*

3   25   degenerano dopo tre secoli in un <u>sensazionalismo</u> frettoloso: *sensazionalismo,* meaning "sensational-ism," is acceptable. But *sensismo,* a word that con-veys the meaning in a more philosophical sense might perhaps be closer to the *mot juste.*

3   25   Si potrebbe dire infatti dell'uomo moderno che ha un'epidermide invece di un'anima. Il potere sensorio del suo organismo si è enormemente sviluppato ma si è sviluppato a pregiudizio della facultà spirituale: This amazing figure of speech and idea might pose a problem to a pedestrian reader.

3   47   Mettete *Tristano ed Isolta* accanto all'*Inferno* e v'accorgerete come l'odio del poeta segue la sua strada d'abisso in abisso nella scia di un idea che s'intensifica e più intensamente il poeta si consuma nel fuoco <u>dell'idea dell'odio</u> più truce diventa l'arte colla quale l'artista ci comunica la sua passione. L'una è un'arte di circostanze, l'altra è ideativa: These are quite complex and original ideas and com-parisons. It is no wonder that they should catch the reader off guard and that she should query them. See Afterword I for more extended explications.

3   56   Il compilatore d'atlanti n<u>el a</u>lto medioevo . . . : The l and the apostrophe are missing. It should be *nell'alto.*

3   62   siamo avidi di ~~dettagli~~ . . . : meaning details or par-ticulars. *Dettagli* is acceptable Italian, though in 1912 *particolari* would have been preferable.

3   63   non parla che di colore locale, dell'<u>am</u>biente . . . : The error here is in dividing the syllables after *l'.* Separation should be between double consonants: *del-l'ambiente.*

Notes on the Thesis-Reader's Corrections

PARAGRAPH	LINE	

3   66   l'accumulazione di ~~dettagli~~ osservati. *Particolari* would probably have been preferable in 1912.

4   3   una fecondità impro<u>v</u>isa . . . : *Improvvisa* is spelled with two *v*'s.

4   59   Difatti, il rinascimento venne quando l'arte periva di perfezione formale ed il pensiero si perdeva in sottigliezze oziose: The question mark near these sentences would seem to be a negative reaction to Joyce's paradoxes.

4   8   Un poema s'era rid<u>otto un</u> problema alge<u>braico</u> . . . : *Ridotto* also takes *a* after it: *ridotta a un problema. Algebrico* is the correct spelling.

5   4   e quantunque i cantori non ci siano più <u>le</u> loro opere sono come le conchiglie marine: The reader might have been calling attention to the need for a comma or some other kind of punctuation between *più* and *le*.

6   3   Tutta la conquista moderna, dell'aria, della terra, del mare, della malattia, dell'ignoranza, si fonde, per così dire, nel crogiuolo della mente e si trasforma in una piccola goccia d'acqua, in una lagrima. Se il rinascimento non avesse fatto altro, avrebbe fatto molto creando in noi stessi e nella nostra arte il senso della pietà per ogni essere che vive . . . : We might harp on long and free flowing or floating phrases here, but it would not be worth it if we missed the poetry or constricted it out of existence.

DISTINCTIVE
or
OBSCURE
WORDS *and* PHRASES
in
JOYCE'S
PADUAN ESSAYS

Note: The numbers given for "paragraph" and "line" refer to the translation of Joyce's Italian essay.

PARAGRAPH LINE

1   1   The theory of evolution . . . grown up: Joyce borrows some phrases in this sentence from the concluding sentences of the first draft version of "Daniel Defoe," his March 1912 lecture at the Università Popolare in Trieste, wherein he says: "Il nostro secolo che ama risalire alle origini dei fenomeni attuali per convincersi ancora una volta della verità della sua dottrina evoluzionista la quale insegna che quando eravamo piccoli non eravamo grandi, potrebbe rileggere la storia di Robinson Crusoe e del suo servitore Venerdì con gran profitto." See Peter Spielberg, *James Joyce's Manuscripts and Letters at the University of Buffalo: A Catalogue* (VII.A.3). The passage may be translated as follows: "Our century, which loves to retrace actual phenomena to their sources in order to convince itself once again of the truth of the theory of evolution, which teaches that when we were little we were not grown up, could reread the story of Robinson Crusoe and his man Friday with great profit." See Joseph Prescott, "Daniel Defoe," *Buffalo Studies,* Vol. II, No. 1, Dec. 1964, for the complete first draft ending in Italian and his translation of it. Prescott also points out a connection between sarcasm directed against overstressing the obvious in the Defoe passage and Stephen's sarcasm in the "Scylla and Charybdis" episodes of *Ulysses:* "Monsieur de la Pallise, Stephen sneered, was alive fifteen minutes before his death" (184). As Joyce ridiculed an evolutionary truism in "Daniel Defoe" and in the Renaissance essay, so does Stephen ridicule Lyster the librarian's and Goethe's truisms on Hamlet.

PARAGRAPH LINE

1   3   the European Renaissance: See Afterword I and a
            discussion of some of Joyce's comments on the
            Renaissance in Power's *Conversations with James
            Joyce* (1974). In "The Bruno Philosophy" (1903)
            Joyce says of Bruno that his system "is full of that
            ardent sympathy with nature as it is—*natura
            naturata*—which is the breath of the Renaissance."
            Critical Writings, p. 133.

1   9   *laudator temporis acti:* "a praiser of times past" from
            Horace, *De Arte Poetica*, 1. 173. Stephen's descrip-
            tion of his father in *A Portrait* includes this allusion
            to Horace's poem: "Stephen began to enumerate
            glibly his father's attributes. —A medical student, an
            oarsman, a tenor, an amateur actor, a shouting politi-
            cian, a small landlord, a small investor, a drinker,
            a good fellow, a storyteller, somebody's secretary,
            something in a distillery, a taxgatherer, a bankrupt
            and at present a praiser of his own past" (241).

1   12   the scattered elements of utility and knowledge:
            See Joyce's review, "Humanism" (1903), a review of
            Humanism: Philosophical Essays by F .C. S. Schiller
            (a follower of William James). In the review, pub-
            lished in the *Daily Express,* Dublin, November 12,
            1903, Joyce states: "Pragmatism is really a very
            considerable thing. It reforms logic, it shows the ab-
            surdity of pure thought, it establishes an ethical
            basis for metaphysic, makes practical usefulness the
            criterion of truth, and pensions off the Absolute
            once and for all. In other words, pragmatism is com-
            mon-sense. The reader, accordingly, will not be sur-
            prised to find that in the post-Platonic dialogue,
            which is called ' "Useless" Knowledge,' a disciple of
            William James utterly routs and puts to shame
            the ghostly forms of Plato and Aristotle." *Critical
            Writings*, pp. 135–36. Joyce's ironic tone runs coun-
            ter to what he is saying and the rest of the review
            is abrasive against Schiller's pragmatist position.

Distinctive or Obscure Words and Phrases in Joyce's Paduan Essays

PARAGRAPH LINE

2   2   against scholastic absolutism, against that immense (and in many respects admirable) philosophical system: Joyce interestingly defended scholasticism to a degree against pragmatism in "Humanism," a review of *Humanism: Philosophical Essays* by F. C. S. Schiller (a follower of William James). In the review, published in the *Daily Express*, Dublin, Nov. 12, 1903, Joyce states: "Barbarism, says Professor Schiller, may show itself in philosophy in two guises, as barbarism of style and as barbarism of temper, and what is opposed to barbarism is Professor Schiller's philosophical creed: Humanism, or, as he sometimes names it, Pragmatism. One, therefore, who has been prepared to expect courteous humanism both in temper and in style, will read with some surprise statements such as—'The *a priori* philosophies have all been found out' . . . 'It [the Dragon of Scholasticism] is a spirit . . . that grovels in muddy technicality, buries itself in the futile burrowings of valuless researches, and conceals itself from human insight [but not from humane insight, Professor Schiller!] by dust-clouds of desiccated rubbish which it raises.' " *Critical Writings*, p. 135.

2   20   as a woman, tired of the peace and quiet that distress her heart, turns her gaze toward the temptations of life: This Bruno-like counterpointing of feelings is echoed by Bloom's ideas in the "Eumaeus" section of *Ulysses*: "He personally, being of a sceptical bias, believed, and didn't make the smallest bones about saying so either, that man, or men in the plural, were always hanging around on the waiting list about a lady, even supposing she was the best wife in the world and they got on fairly well together for the sake of argument, when, neglecting her duties, she chose to be tired of wedded life, and was on for a little flutter in polite debauchery to

PARAGRAPH   LINE

press their attentions on her with improper intent,
the upshot being that her affections centred on another, the cause of many *liaisons* between still
attractive married women getting on for fair and
forty and younger men, no doubt as several famous
cases of feminine infatuation proved up to the hilt"
(655–66).

2   22   Giordano Bruno himself says that every power,
whether in nature or in the spirit, must create an opposite power . . . reunion: Ellmann in *James Joyce*
tells us that Father Ghezzi, S.J., at University College, Dublin, first introduced Joyce to the works of
Bruno (1548–1600). Bruno, along with Galileo,
Sarpi, and Campanella, is often considered to be a
major champion of freedom in 16th century Italy.
Kepler and Copernicus influenced his thought; he
envisaged an infinity of creation beyond the solar
system in which the divine spirit was manifest. In
A Portrait Stephen notes in his diary: "Then went
to College. Other wrangle with little roundhead
rogue'seye Ghezzi. This time about Bruno the
Nolan. Began in Italian and ended in pidgin English.
He said Bruno was a terrible heretic. I said he was
terribly burned. He agreed to this with some sorrow"
(249). See Weldon Thornton, *Allusions in ULYSSES*
(397) for similar references to Bruno in *Stephen
Hero* and *Ulysses*. See Ellmann, *Ulysses on the
Liffey*, on Joyce's thematic and structural uses of
Bruno's ideas on opposing forces and their reunions
in *Ulysses*. See Adaline Glasheen, *A Second Census
of FINNEGANS WAKE*, for Joyce's many references
to Bruno in the *Wake*; also James Atherton, *The
Books at the Wake*. Bruno and his being burnt at the
stake are incorporated as a *ricorso* in Vico's system
of cycles in the *Wake* along with Quinet, Michelet,
and Giambattista Vico himself: "If juness she saved!
A ho! And if yulone he pouved! The ol old stolio-

lum! From quiqui quinet to michemiche chelet and a jambebatiste to a brulobrulo!" (117.12).

3   10   the journalist in the monk's chair: that is to say, has deposed an acute, limited and formal mentality to give the scepter to a mentality that is facile and wide-ranging . . . amorphous mentality: This passage seems to be relevant to *A Portrait of the Artist as a Young Man* in respect to Stephen's using the "acute, limited and formal mentality" of Thomistic thought in organizing his religious life in Chapters III and IV and then in Chapter V in resolving esthetic questions. His mind in Chapter V at various times is described as being monklike and cloistral. An ironic scene in the library portrays Dixon reading a chess problem to Cranly from a journal and disturbing a priest who is reading *The Tablet,* a conservative Roman Catholic weekly newspaper published in England. The import of the passage from the Renaissance essay does seem to be even more resonant in *Ulysses,* particularly in the "Aeolus" episode, where Stephen's acute mind is contrasted with the amorphous mentalities of the journalists and the hangers-on at the newspaper offices and their levels of speech and the levels of writing that get published in the papers. Stuart Gilbert lists four pages of different kinds of rhetoric employed. The journalists are very evidently in the monk's chair and their facile, wide-ranging, restless, and amorphous natures are captured by Bloom who thinks: "Myles Crawford began on the *Independent.* Funny the way those newspaper men veer about when they get wind of a new opening. Weathercocks. Hot and cold in the same breath. Wouldn't know which to believe. One story good till you hear the next. Go for one another bald-headed in the papers and then all blows over. Hail-fellow well met the next moment" (125). When Lenehan enters the inner office with Sports tissues,

PARAGRAPH LINE

he touts "Sceptre" as a certain winner for the Gold Cup horserace. Sceptre in this context might represent Thomistic thought, a horse that loses to "Throwaway," who might represent the journalist to whom the Renaissance, as Joyce puts it in his essay, has given "the sceptre."

3   13   Shakespeare and Lope de Vega . . . cinematography. The untiring creative force . . . frenetic sensationalism: This passage somewhat echoes Joyce's remarks on Shakespeare and Lope de Vega in his Trieste lecture on Daniel Defoe of March 1912: "Shakespeare, with his Titianesque palette, his flow of language, his epileptic passionateness, and his creative fury, is an Italianate Englishman, while the Restoration theater takes its cue from the Spanish theater, from the works of Calderon and Lope de Vega." "Daniel Defoe," ed. from Italian manuscripts and trans. by Joseph Prescott. *Buffalo Studies*, pub. by SUNY at Buffalo, Vol. I, No. 1, Dec., 1964, p. 7. Joyce's point in "Daniel Defoe" is that Defoe was the first English author to write without literary models and is the "father of the English novel." His characters express the true national spirit of England. Shakespeare, according to Joyce, did not capture the English soul, as English *per se* or Anglo-Saxon, other than in his peasants, strolling players, fools, and gravediggers. Most of his heroes were foreigners. His monarchs were Normans, Plantagenets, Tudors—all Celts who ruled over England until William of Orange restored Anglo-Saxon blood to the English throne in 1688, which was, coincidentally or not, a date that but shortly preceded the emergence of Defoe's literary works. The Italian Renaissance may have permeated Shakespeare, and the Spanish Renaissance may have permeated the Restoration theater, but the English soul and character permeated Defoe. Yet I may note, the scepter

passed on to the journalist in the Renaissance was also passed on to Defoe, who, as Joyce explains, founded one of the first English newspapers, *The Review*, while still in jail and was "the great precursor" of the realist movement. In another passage from "Daniel Defoe" Joyce relates a Defoe novel to the cinema (perhaps an adumbration of his relating Shakespeare's and Vega's plays to it in his Renaissance essay) and journalism: "The Spanish chapters of the *Memoirs of Captain Carleton*, on the other hand, crammed with gallant adventures, bullfights, and executions, are, as today's film jargon would have it, taken from life. If Defoe were still alive, by his gifts of exactitude and imagination, by his farraginous experience, and by his neat, precise style he would probably enjoy great fame as special correspondent of some mammoth American or English newspaper." "Daniel Defoe," *op. cit.*, p. 20.

3   22   The most characteristic literary works we possess are simply amoral: See Afterword I. It may be reiterated that Joyce expressed concern for moral values in literature in a fragment of a letter to his brother Stanislaus of July 19, 1905. Goldsmith rears the flower of *The Vicar of Wakefield* from the putridity of his age, whereas Maupassant and contemporary Irish writers are "morally obtuse." A section from the fragment is quite important to place the above quotation in context: "The preface to *The Vicar of Wakefield* which I read yesterday gave me a moment of doubt as to the excellence of my literary manners." The Preface to *The Vicar of Wakefield* is brief and is quoted here in full: "There are a hundred faults in this thing, and a hundred things might be said to prove them beauties. But it is needless. A book may be amusing with numerous errors, or it may be very dull without a single absurdity. The hero of this piece unites in himself the

three greatest characters on earth: he is a priest, a husbandman, and the father of a family. He is drawn as ready to teach and ready to obey; as simple in affluence, and majestic in adversity. In this age of opulence and refinement, whom can such a character please? Such as are fond of high life, will turn with disdain from the simplicity of his country fireside. Such as mistake ribaldry for humour, will find no wit in his harmless conversation; and such as have been taught to deride religion, will laugh at one whose chief stores of comfort are drawn from futurity."

3   23   (*The Crisis* of Marco Praga): A part of Joyce's inventory of the books he left behind him in Trieste in 1915 includes four titles by Marco Praga (1862–1929): Shelf 3, Front, No. 34. *La Biondina* (novel); No. 35. *Le Vergini* (play in four acts); No. 36. *Alleluja* (play in three acts); No. 37. *La Moglie ideale* (play in three acts). See Ellmann, *James Joyce*, p. 794. Gianni Pinguentini in *James Joyce in Italia* draws some inferences about another book on the list, Shelf 3, Back, No. 2., Bracciforte's *Chiave dei temi scenegiatti.* The title in English is *Keys to Scenic Themes.* Pinguentini relates the book to Praga's writings and praises Praga as a prolific comic dramatist of the eighties who was inventive as a writer of crude *verismo*. He states that Joyce used him while working on *Exiles* or some other projected dramatic work. He also says that Giacosa thought highly of Praga. Critics have generally considered *The Crisis* to be Praga's best work.

3   24   *Pelléas et Mélisande* of Maeterlinck: Joyce discusses dramatic qualities in Maeterlinck (1862–1949) in his essay "Ecce Homo" (1899): "Maeterlinck's characters may be, when subjected to the search-light of that estimable torch, common sense, unac-

countable, drifting, fate-impelled creatures—in fact, as our civilization dubs them, uncanny. But in whatever dwarfed and marionette-like a manner, their passions are human, and so the exposition of them is drama." *Critical Writings,* p. 32. He taunts the directors of the Irish Literary Theatre and Mélisande in "The Day of the Rabblement" (1901): "Earnest dramatists of the second rank, Sudermann, Bjornson, and Giacosa, can write very much better plays than the Irish Literary Theatre has staged. But, of course, the directors would not like to present such improper writers to the uncultivated, much less to the cultivated, rabblement. Accordingly, the rabblement, placid and intensely moral, is enthroned in boxes and galleries amid a hum of approval—*la bestia Trionfante*—and those who think Echegaray is 'morbid', and titter coyly when Mélisande lets down her hair, are not sure but they are the trustees of every intellectual and poetic treasure." *Critical Writings,* p. 70.

3 24 *Crainquebille* of Anatole France: Joyce read France's novel *Crainquebille* in Rome. In his letter of December 7, 1906, to Stanislaus in Trieste he praises the work: "Crainquebele, of course, is very fine and parts or rather phrases, of his other books." In this novella the main character Crainquebille is arrested and imprisoned for a crime he did not commit—that of saying *Morte aux vaches* ("Kill the cops") to a cop. The expression literally means "Kill the cows." Police were associated with cows because they stood idly around like them. The phrase, in its literal sense of "Kill the cows," relates to the hoof-and-mouth disease in *Ulysses* and particularly to the violation of fertility theme in "The Oxen of the Sun" episode. Frank Costello uses the expression *Morte aux vaches* there in the style of Daniel Defoe (author of *A Journal of the Plague Year*) in response to Lenehan's

PARAGRAPH LINE

comments on the hoof-and-mouth disease. The two libertines discuss the issue as follows: "The other, Costello, that is, hearing this talk asked was it poetry or a tale. Faith, no, he says, Frank (that was his name), 'tis all about Kerry cows that are to be butchered along of the plague. But they can go hang, says he with a wink, for me with their bully beef, a pox on it . . . *Morte aux vaches,* says Frank then in the French language that had been indentured to a brandy shipper that has a winelodge in Bordeaux and he spoke French like a gentleman too" (398). Joyce comments on Anatole France's "cutting style" within a larger vista that sees modern French realism in conflict with France's (the country's) spiritual roots in "Daniel Defoe": "Modern realism is perhaps a reaction. The great French nation, which venerates the legend of the Maid of Orleans, nevertheless disfigures her through the mouth of Voltaire, lasciviously defiles her in the hands of the engravers of the nineteenth century, riddles and shreds her in the twentieth century with the cutting style of Anatole France. The very intensity, the very refinement of French realism betray its spiritual origins." Translated by Joseph Prescott, *op. cit.,* pp. 22–23.

3 25 *Smoke* of Turgenev: This novel was first published in the March issue of *The Russian Messenger* in 1867. In a letter from Rome to Stanislaus Joyce in Trieste of December 1906, Joyce indicates that he has read a French translation of *Smoke, Fumée,* but does not share Stanislaus's appreciation of it or of Turgenev's *A Sportsman's Notebook.*

3 27 A great modern artist: This allusion is to Richard Wagner, the composer of the opera *Tristan und Isolde* (1859). Bloom thinks his music is "grand" but "a bit too heavy" in the "Eumaeus" episode of

Ulysses. It is also "hard to follow at the first go-off" for him (661).

3   27   wishing to put the sentiment of love to music reproduces . . . each pulsation, each trembling, the lightest shivering, the lightest sigh . . . their bodies become one single flesh: This view of Wagner's love scenes, perhaps that of the *Liebestod,* seems to echo some of the attacks against Wagner in Max Nordau's chapter "The Richard Wagner cult" in his book *Degeneration,* published in 1895. Nordau says that Wagner is "a declared anarchist" and an "erotic (in a psychiatric sense)." He quotes from Wagner's *Art-Work of the Future* wherein Wagner imagines the arts of dancing, music, and poetry as three muses dancing: " '. . . now the one entranced by a backward glance at the twin forms of her closely entwined sisters, bending towards them; then two, carried away by the allurements of the one [!] greeting her in homage; finally all, in close embrace, breast to breast, limb to limb, in an ardent kiss of love, coalescing in one blissfully living shape. This is the love and life, the joy and wooing of art,' etc." Nordau comments: "(Observe the word-play: *Lieben und Leben, Freuen und Freien!*) Wagner here visibly loses the thread of his argument; he neglects what he really wishes to say, and revels in the picture of the three dancing maidens, who have arisen before his mind's eye, following with lascivious longing the outline of their forms and their seductive movements." Joyce in his essay says "one single flesh"; Nordau quotes Wagner's "one blissfully living shape." Nordau says Wagner loses the thread of his thought as he follows "with lascivious longing" the seductive movements; Joyce says Wagner's art is not ideational. The similarities are close, and they seem to become closer when Nordau discusses the erotic qualities of his operas, *Rhein-*

gold, Siegfried, and the *Walküre.* His "The amorous
whinings, whimperings and raving of *Tristan und
Isolde"* sounds close to Joyce's comments on
Wagner and *Tristan.* If so, it is quite a comment
on Joyce's eclectic-intellectual range. Even though
Nordau attacks the French Symbolist poets and
other inspirers of Joyce's aesthetic views as degenerate criminal minds that try to pass for artists,
Joyce persisted in his habit of borrowing ideas that
meant something to him without accepting the overall context in which they appeared. Joyce alludes to
Wagner and *Tristan* somewhat with the attitude and
tone of his Renaissance essay in regarding Glugg
as an exile and writer in *Finnegans Wake:* "the best
and schortest way of blacking out a caughtalock of
all the sorrors of Sexton until he would accoster her
coume il fou in teto-dous as a wagoner would his
mudheeldy wheesindonk at their trist in Parisise
after tourments of tosend years, bread cast out on
waters, making goods at mutuurity, Mondamoiseau
of Casanuova and Mademoisselle from Armentières"
(230). "wheesindonk" is an allusion to Wagner's
mistress Mathilde Wesendonk, who inspired *Tristan
und Isolde.*

3   38   art of circumstance: See Afterword I. Also see
Baudelaire's chapter, "Le Peintre de la Vie Moderne"
in *L'Art Romantique* on the fusion of essential and
eternal qualities of beauty and circumstances of
beauty. This chapter has been published as a separate book with illustrations of C. G.'s paintings and
sketches, *The Painter of Victorian Life: A Study of
Constantin Guys* with an introduction and a translation of Baudelaire's "Peintre de la Vie Moderne"
by P. G. Konody, ed. by C. Geoffrey Holme (London: The Studio Ltd., 1930). Baudelaire makes a
quite provocative statement that relates to *Ulysses*
and *Finnegans Wake:* "The Beautiful consists of an

Distinctive or Obscure Words and Phrases in Joyce's Paduan Essays

eternal, invarible element, the quantity of which it
is exceedingly difficult to determine, and of a relative, circumstantial element, which may be, as you
please, in turn or simultaneously, the epoch, the
fashion, morality or passion. Without this second
element, which is, as it were, the amusing, titillating,
appetising envelope of the divine sweet, the first element would be indigestible, unappreciable, not
adapted and not appropriate to human nature. I
defy you to discover any example of beauty that
does not contain these two elements" (p. 24).
Compare this with the discussion of rainstorms,
raincoats, umbrellas, and nudity in "The Oxen
of the Sun" in *Ulysses* (405) and the discussion of
the letter in the *Wake:* "Has any fellow, of the
dime a dozen type . . . ever looked sufficiently
longly at a quite everydaylooking stamped addressed
envelope? Admittedly it is an outer husk: its face,
in all its featureful perfection of imperfection, is its
fortune: it exhibits only the civil or military clothing of whatever passionpallid nudity or plague-
purple nakedness may happen to tuck itself under its
flap. Yet to concentrate solely on the literal sense
or even the psychological content of any document
to the sore neglect of the enveloping facts themselves circumstantiating it is just as hurtful to sound
sense (and let it be added to the truest taste) as
were some fellow in the act of perhaps getting an
intro from another fellow turning out to be a friend
in need of his, say, to a lady of the latter's acquaint-
ance, engaged in performing the elaborative ante-
cistral ceremony of upstheres, straightaway to run
off and vision her plump and plain in her natural
altogether, preferring to close his blinkhards' eyes
to the ethiquethical fact that she was, after all,
wearing for the space of the time being some defi-
nite articles of evolutionary clothing, inharmonious

creations, a captious critic might describe them as, or not strictly necessary or a trifle irritating here and there, but for all that suddenly full of local colour and personal perfume and suggestive, too, of so very much more and capable of being stretched, filled out, if need or wish were, of having their surprisingly like coincidental parts separated don't they now, for better survey by the deft hand of an expert, don't you know?" (109.1–30). Baudelaire also makes much of clothing and beauty in his chapter as Joyce does in the above passage and as he continues to do in the sentences that follow the passage.

4   5   A poem was reduced to an alegbraic problem: Cf: Mulligan's comment to Haines in Chapter I of *Ulysses* about Stephen's interpretation of *Hamlet:* "It's quite simple. He proves by algebra that Hamlet's grandson is Shakespeare's grandfather and that he himself is the ghost of his own father" (18).

4   7   A philosopher was an erudite sophist like Bellarmine: St. Robert Bellarmine, S. J. (1542–1621) wrote *Disputations on the Controversies* in four volumes between 1576 and 1587 as a defense of the Church largely based on St. Thomas. He is more widely known for his admonishments against his friend Galileo and his theories. He entered the University of Padua as a student in 1565.

4   7   A philosopher was an erudite sophist like . . . Giovanni Mariana who, while yet preaching the word of Jesus to the masses, endeavored to construct a moral defense for tyrannicide: Stephen refers to Mariana (a Spanish Jesuit, historian and theologian: 1536–1624) in *A Portrait* in response to Cranly's question which Stephen interprets as eliciting a sophist's answer:

Distinctive or Obscure Words and Phrases in Joyce's Paduan Essays

PARAGRAPH LINE

"—You wish me to say, Stephen answered, that the rights of property are provisional and that in certain circumstances it is not unlawful to rob. Everyone would act in that belief. So I will not make you that answer. Apply to the jesuit theologian Juan Mariana de Talavera who will also explain to you in what circumstances you may lawfully kill your king and whether you had better hand him his poison in a goblet or smear it for him upon his robe or his saddlebow. Ask me rather would I suffer others to rob me or, if they did, would I call down upon them what I believe is called the chastisemant of the secular arm?

—And would you?

—I think, Stephen said, it would pain me as much to do so as to be robbed" (246).

Note: The numbers given for "paragraph" and "line" refer to the printed version of the Dickens essay, not to the holograph.

PARAGRAPH LINE

1   6   The form he chose to write in, diffuse, overloaded with minute and often irrelevant observations . . . greatest conviction: In this comment on Dickens, Joyce seems to see his work as an example of art of circumstance which he discussed in the Renaissance essay and implied was not of as high an order as ideational art.

2   8   If Dickens is to move you, you must not allow him to stray out of hearing of the chimes of Bow Bells: Bow bells refers to the bells of Bow Church or St. Mary-le-Bow Church, formerly Seyn Marie Church of the Arches, in Cheapside, London, nearly in the center of the city. It was called Bow because of the "bows" or arches that supported its steeple and a lantern in its tower. The church was destroyed in the Great Fire of London (1666), and later rebuilt by Sir Christopher Wren. It is celebrated for the peal of its bells. According to the *OED* the phrase "within the sound of Bow-bells" has come to be synonymous with "within the City bounds." This reference connects in the essay with the story of Dick Whittington who thought he heard the Bow bells telling him "Turn again, Whittington, thrice Lord Mayor of London," when he was running away.

2   20   *Barnaby Rudge* . . . not unworthy of being placed beside the *Journal of the Plague* of Defoe: In "Daniel Defoe," Joyce's Trieste lecture of March 1912, Joyce describes various scenes from the *Journal of the Plague Year*. A segment of one of Joyce's descriptions reads: "Behind the church in Aldgate an enormous pit was dug. Here the carters unloaded the

PARAGRAPH LINE

wagons and threw pitiful lime on the heaps of
blackened corpses. The desperate and the criminal
caroused in the taverns day and night. The dying
ran to cast themselves among the dead. Pregnant
women howled for help. Great smoking fires burned
continuously at street corners and in the public
squares. Religious frenzy reached the highest pitch.
One madman, with a pan of burning charcoal on
his head, quite naked, paced the street crying that
he was a prophet and continually repeating, 'O the
great and the dreadful God!' " "Daniel Defoe," ed.
and trans. by Joseph Prescott, *Buffalo Studies*, Vol.
I, No. 1, Dec. 1964, pp. 16–17. Joyce adds that the
saddler's narrative of the horrors is masterly and
orchestral "which reminds one of Tolstoy's *Sevas-
topol* or Hauptmann's *Weavers*. But in these two
works we are aware of a lyric surge, a self-conscious
art, a musical theme which would appear to be the
emotional revolt of modern man against human or
superhuman iniquity. In Defoe there is nothing
of the kind: neither lyricism nor art for art's sake
nor social consciousness." P. 17. The saddler's narra-
tion results from his ordinary observations and experiences as he walks along the street. The orchestral
quality of Dickens's description of the mob surging
forward and backward, stampeding and stopping in
Barnaby Rudge may perhaps be worthy of comparison with Joyce's choice descriptions of the *Journal
of the Plague Year*.

2   27   English country of "meadows trim with daisies
pied": Milton, "L'Allegro," 1. 75.

"Meadows trim with daisies pied,
Shallow brooks, and rivers wide.
Towers and battlements it sees
Bosom'd high in tufted trees,
Where perhaps some Beauty lies,
The Cynosure of neighbouring eyes."

PARAGRAPH LINE

Joyce and Dickens concentrated on city life, as opposed to country life, because they knew it well, but also, perhaps, because they sensed that the cities dominated ˋmodern life. Power tells Joyce in Chapter XIII of *Conversations with James Joyce* that he likes Lamartine's "Graziella," set in the open air on the Mediterranean shore. Power says about "Graziella": "And it is a pleasant contrast to the modern books which are mostly urban, about the artificial life that is lived in towns and cities." Joyce answers him: "That is because cities are of primary interest nowadays. . . . This is the period of urban domination. The modern advance in techniques has made them so." Dickens and Joyce enjoy the countryside, but it could only be a background for both of them as serious city novelists.

2   30   could Dickens have applied to himself Lord Palmerston's famous *Civis Romanus sum*: E. Cobham Brewer in *A Handbook of Phrase and Fable* (a frequent reference for Joyce) has the following entry for *Civis Romanus sum*: " 'I am a Roman citizen', a plea which sufficed to stop arbitrary condemnation, bonds, and scourging. No Roman citizen could be condemned unheard; by the Valerian Law he could not be bound; by the Sempronian Law it was forbidden to scourge him or beat him with rods. When the chief captain commanded PAUL 'should be examined by scourging', he asked, 'Is it lawful for you to scourge a man that is a Roman, and uncondemned?' " (Acts, xxii, 24–25). See also Acts xvi, 37, etc.

The phrase gained an English fame from the peroration of Palmerston's great speech in the House of Commons (24 June, 1850) over the Don Pacifico affair: " 'As the Roman, in days of old, held himself free from indignity, when he could say *Civis Romanus sum*, so also a British subject, in

PARAGRAPH LINE

whatever land he may be, shall feel confident that the watchful eye and the strong arm of England will protect him against injustice and wrong.' "

2 31 The noble lord, to tell the truth, succeeded on that memorable occasion (as Gladstone, unless my memory misleads me, took care to point out) in saying the opposite of what he had in mind to say. Wishing to say that he was an imperialist he said that he was a Little Englander: G. Barnett Smith in his *The Life of the Right Honourable William Ewart Gladstone* (1881) comments on Gladstone's speech in response to Palmerston and quotes from it. Smith says: "Non-interference had been laid down as the basis of our conduct towards other nations; but the policy of Lord Palmerston had been characterised by a spirit of active interference." An excerpt from Gladstone's speech, as quoted by Smith, is: "And now I will grapple with the noble lord on the ground which he selected for himself, in the most triumphant portion of his speech, by his reference to those emphatic words, *Civis Romanus sum*. He vaunted, amidst the cheers of his supporters, that under his administration an Englishman should be, throughout the world, what the citizen of Rome had been. What then, sir, was a Roman citizen? He was the member of a privileged caste; he belonged to a conquering race, to a nation that held all others bound down by the strong arm of power. For him there was to be an exceptional system of law; for him principles were to be asserted, and by him rights were to be enjoyed, that were denied to the rest of the world" (p. 115).

2 37 The church bells . . . seem to have called him back . . . like another Whittington, promising him (and the promise was to be amply fulfilled) a three-fold greatness: The church bells are those of Bow

PARAGRAPH   LINE

Church which seemed to tell Richard "Dick" Whittington (1358?–1423), while running away from the cook who mistreated him and resting in Holloway, "Turn again, Whittington, thrice Lord Mayor of London." He did turn back to his master Fitzwarren and was elected Mayor three times. E. Cobham Brewer in *The Reader's Handbook* (1891) relates the story as follows: "Whittington (Dick), a poor orphan country lad, who heard that London was 'paved with gold,' and went there to get a living. When reduced to starving point, a kind merchant gave him employment in his family to help the cook, but the cook so ill treated him that he ran away. Sitting to rest himself on the roadside, he heard Bow Bells, and they seemed to him to say, 'Turn again, Whittington, thrice lord Mayor of London;' so he returned to his master. By-and-by the master allowed him, with the other servants, to put in an adventure in a ship bound for Morocco. Richard had nothing but a cat, which, however, he sent. Now it happened that the king of Morocco was troubled by mice, which Whittington's cat destroyed; and this so pleased his highness that he bought the mouser at a fabulous price. Dick commenced business with this money, soon rose to great wealth, married his master's daughter, was knighted, and thrice elected lord Mayor of London—in 1398, 1406, and 1419."

2   56   One is curious to know how the great Cockney would fare at the hands of R.L.S. or of Mr Kipling or of Mr George Moore: Dickens fared fairly well in the hands of Robert Louis Stevenson, very well in those of Kipling, and not so well in those of Moore. George Ford tells us in *Dickens and His Readers: Aspects of Novel Criticism since 1836* that Stevenson did not often speak of Dickens; but "that he disliked such novels as *Bleak House* but

 2 56 admired *Our Mutual Friend.* The 'fierce intensity
of design' in the portrait of Bradley Headstone he
considered to be 'one of Dickens's superlative
achievements.' " P. 203. Dickens had a direct influence on Kipling, who predicted that he would become
more modern as time passed. He was also indirectly
influenced by the American Dickensian and local
colorist, Bret Harte. Moore read Dickens extensively,
but as a follower of Zola and Flaubert did not appreciate his humor. Moore said that Dickens "had more
talent than Flaubert, Zola, Goncourt, Daudet; but he
would have learnt from them the value of serious-
ness. . . . He would have learnt that humour is more
commercial than literary." *Avowals* (N.Y., 1923),
p. 79, as quoted by Ford, *op. cit.,* pp. 217–18. Mulligan, in *Ulysses,* quips on George Moore's party that
he and Eglington plan to attend that night—"Monsieur Moore, he said, lecturer on French letters to the
youth of Ireland. I'll be there" (214–15). Stephen
thinks: "Swill till eleven. Irish nights' entertain-
ment." He is not invited to hear Moore, but rather
hears Mulligan recapitulate Moore's stories at the
party in "Oxen of the Sun" that suggests a "con-
traceptive" view of Moore's style and Mulligan's
sexual proclivities; both may be contrasted with
Dickens's sentimental but fertile style, which Joyce
uses to dramatize the birth of Nina Purefoy's baby.
Joyce in the essay does assign Dickens "a place
among the great literary creators," pending judg-
ments from Stevenson, Kipling, and Moore.

 3 7 a great caricaturist in the sense that Hogarth is:
John Forster in *The Life of Charles Dickens* com-
pares Dickens and Hogarth and quotes Dickens on
Hogarth. See Vol. II, Book 6, Chp. III, "Seaside
Holidays," pp. 41–43. Dickens's comments on "The
Rake's Progress," "Marriage-a-la-Mode," and "Gin
Lane." The drunken woman sprawled out near the

pawn-broker's shop in "Gin Lane" may have been a source for Stephen Blackpool's wife, who pawns her furniture to buy liquor in *Hard Times* (1854): which may be in turn a literary source for Martin Cunningham's drunken wife who pawns her furniture to buy liquor in *Ulysses*. See Afterword II for close textual connections between *Hard Times* and *Ulysses*. Jaun in his sermon to the 29 girls in *Finnegans Wake*, III, iii, seems to moralize in a Hogarthian and Dickensian way against their following "The Harlot's Progress." On 433.15–20 Jaun cautions against flirty ways: "Make a strong point of never kicking up your rumpus over the scroll end of sofas in Dar Bey Coll Cafeteria by tootling risky *apropos* songs at commercial travellers' smokers for their Columbian nights entertainments the like of *White limbs they never stop teasing* or *Minxy was a Manxmaid when Murry wor a Man*." Dickens's Pleasant Riderhood, Rogue Riderhood's twenty-four-year-old daughter, in *Our Mutual Friend* and Dora Spenlow, daughter of Mr. Spenlow in *David Copperfield*, seem to be punned on in 434.6–10 in another of Jaun's warnings: "Recollect the yella perals that all too often beset green gerils, Rhidarhoda and Daradora, once they gethobbyhorsical, playing breeches parts for Bessy Sudlow in flesh-coloured pantos instead of earthing down in the coalhole trying to boil the big gun's dinner." (Bessy Sudlow, a Dublin actress, was married to Michael Gunne.) The Riderhoods, father and daughter, lived in "Limehouse Hole." There seems to be a more direct allusion to Hogarth's "A Harlot's Progress" in 434.14–19: "Remember the biter's bitters I shed the vigil I buried our Harlotte Quai from poor Mrs Mangain's of Britain Court on the feast of Marie Maudlin. Ah, who would wipe her weeper dry and lead her to the halter? Sold in her heyday, laid in the straw, bought for one puny petunia. Moral: if you can't point a lily get to henna out of here!" Allusions to Thackeray's *Vanity Fair* and Dickens's *Pickwick* (Rachael Wardle's elopement), *Martin Chuzzlewit* (cruel and cunning Jonas Chuzzlewit and Martin), *Our Mutual Friend, David Copperfield* (Uriah Heep), and *The Old Curiosity Shop* appear in Jaun's admonitions also against Issy's becoming a rake on 434.24–33: "Vanity flee and Verity fear! Diobell! Whalebones and buskbutts may hurt you (thwackaway thwuck!) but never lay bare your breast secret (dickette's place!) to joy a Jonas in the Dolphin's Barncar with your meetual fan, Doveyed Covetfilles, comepulsing paynattention spasms between the averthisment for Ulikah's wine and a pair of pulldoors of the old cupiosity shape. There you'll fix your eyes darkled on the autocart of the bringfast cable but here till youre martimorphysed please sit still face to face." Phiz, Dickens's etcher, and Joyce's often-used expression for *face*, is punned on in "martimor*physed* . . . face to face." A direct reference to Hogarth and perhaps the lascivious paintings that hang on the walls in his "Marriage à la Mode" sequence follow directly in 435.5–9. Jaun imagines Algernon Swinburne, "Autist Algy," asking the girls: "won't you be an artist's moral and pose in your nudies as a local esthetic before voluble old masters, introducing you, left to right the party comprises, to hogarths like Bottisilly and Titteretto and Vergognese and Coraggio with their extrahand Mazzaccio, plus the usual bilker's dozen of dowdycameramen."

3   12   fundamentally natural and probable with just one strange, wilful, wayward moral or physical deformity which upsets the equipoise: When Stephen wonders about his "girlfriend" Emma Clery's actions in *A Portrait*, he uses two words, "strange" and

PARAGRAPH   LINE

"wilful" that Joyce had used to describe Dickens's characters: "And if he had judged her harshly? If her life were a simple rosary of hours, her life simple and strange as a bird's life, gay in the morning, restless all day, tired at sundown? Her heart simple and wilful as a bird's heart?" (216). Shortly after his dream of her he repeats the words, almost as incantation of her spirit as the source for the inspiration of his: "An afterglow deepened within his spirit, whence the white flame had passed, deepening to a rose and ardent light. That rose and ardent light was her strange wilful heart, strange that no man had known or would know, wilful from before the beginning of the world: and lured by that ardent roselike glow the choirs of the seraphim were falling from heaven" (217). Stephen uses the word "wayward" to describe his confessions to Cranly when he begins to suspect there is something between Emma and him: "Did that explain his friend's listless silence, his harsh comments, the sudden intrusions of rude speech with which he had shattered so often Stephen's ardent wayward confessions?" (232).

3   24   with that quaint spirit of nice and delicate observation with which we see the pilgrims at the Tabard Inn: Joyce also refers to Chaucer to contrast him with Defoe in his Trieste lecture "Daniel Defoe," where his point is that Defoe was the first English author to express the English, not the foreigner's soul. "Now, too, for the first time the true English soul begins to reveal itself in literature. Consider how infinitesimal the importance of that soul had been in former ages. In Chaucer, a court poet with a polished and elegant style, the native soul hardly stands out as the frame in which are set the adventures of respectable people, that is to say, the Norman clerics and foreign heroes." P. 6.

PARAGRAPH   LINE

3   27   No, we see every character of Dickens in the light of
            one strongly-marked or even exaggerated moral or
            physical quality . . . melancholy: Some connections
            can be made between Joyce's general insights and
            specific characters in Dickens. Sleepiness? Joe, the
            fat boy in *Pickwick Papers* and Hugh, the Ostler
            at the Maypole Inn in *Barnaby Rudge*. There are
            usually two or more referents that Joyce might have
            had in mind. Whimsical self-assertiveness? Sam
            Weller and Jingle in *Pickwick*, Herbert Pocket in
            Great Expectations, and the Artful Dodger in *Oliver
            Twist*, among others. Monstrous obesity? Sam
            Weller's father Tony in *Pickwick* and John Willet in
            Barnaby Rudge. Reptile-like servility? Uriah Heep
            in *David Copperfield* and James Carker in *Dombey
            and Son*. Intense round-eyed stupidity? Maggy,
            Mrs. Bangham's twenty-eight-year-old granddaugh-
            ter in *Little Dorrit* and Barnaby Rudge himself.
            Tearful and absurd melancholy? Mrs. Gummidge in
            David Copperfield.

3   38   To say this of him is really to give him what I think
            they call in that land of strange phrases, America, a
            billet for immortality: Joyce's interest in Ameri-
            canisms was not cursory. In a letter to his nephew
            David Fleischman of August 8, 1937, Joyce men-
            tions that he is sending him a copy of *Huckleberry
            Finn*. Joyce's instructions are specific. He wants
            David to give an account of the plot, and "to mark
            with blue pencil in the margin the most important
            passages of the plot itself and in red pencil here and
            there wherever the words or dialogue seem to call
            for the special attention of a European." He adds:
            "Don't care about spoiling the book. It is a cheap
            edition. If you can then return it to me soon I shall
            try to use whatever bears upon what I am doing."
            Letters, Vol. III, pp. 401–402.

Selected
Bibliography

Adams, R. M. "Hades" in *James Joyce's ULYSSES: Critical Essays.* Edited by Clive Hart and David Hayman. Berkeley, Los Angeles, and London: University of California Press, 1974.

Atherton, James S. *The Books at the Wake: A Study of Literary Allusions in James Joyce's FINNEGANS WAKE.* Carbondale and Edwardsville: Southern Illinois University Press and London and Amsterdam: Feffer and Simons, 1959.

Baudelaire, Charles. "Le Peintre de la Vie Moderne" in *L'Art Romantique.* Notice, Notes et Eclaircissements de M. Jacques Crepet. Paris: Louis Conard, Libraire-Editeur, 1875.

―――. *The Painter of Victorian Life: A Study of Constantin Guys.* Translation and Introduction by P. F. Konody of "Le Peintre de la Vie Moderne." Edited by C. Geoffrey Holme. London: The Studio Ltd., 1930.

Bornstein, George. *Yeats and Shelley.* Chicago and London: University of Chicago Press, 1970.

Budgen, Frank. *James Joyce and the Making of ULYSSES.* Introduction by Hugh Kenner. Bloomington and London: Indiana University Press, 1967.

Chesterton, Gilbert Keith. *Appreciations and Criticisms of the Works of Charles Dickens.* London: Dent and New York: Dutton, 1911.

―――. *Charles Dickens: A Critical Study.* New York: Dodd Mead, 1906.

Crise, Stelio. *Epiphanies & Phadographs: Joyce e Trieste.* Milano: All'Insegna del Pesce D'Oro, 1967.

Delattre, Floris. *De Byron à Francis Thompson.* Paris: Librairie Payot, 1913.

―――. "Le Centenaire de Charles Dickens." *La Revue Pedagogique,* January 1912.

―――. *Dickens et la France: ETUDE D'UNE INTERACTION LITTERAIRE ANGLO-FRANÇAISE.* Paris: Librairie Universitaire, J. Gambier, Editeur, 1929.

Dickens, Charles. *Dickens' Works*. New Century Edition. Boston: Dana Estes and Co., 1900.

Dismukes, William Paul. "Michelet and Vico: A Study of Michelet's Use of Vichian Principles." An Abstract of a Doctoral Thesis at the University of Illinois. Urbana, 1936.

Dujardin, Edouard. *We'll To the Woods No More*. Translation of *Les lauriers sont coupés* by Stuart Gilbert, Introduction by Leon Edel, and Illustrations by Alice Laughlin. New York: New Directions, 1938 and 1957.

Eliot, T. S. "Wilkie Collins and Dickens." *Selected Essays*. New York: Harcourt, Brace, 1950.

Ellmann, Richard. *The Consciousness of James Joyce*. New York: Oxford University Press, 1977.

———. *The Identity of Yeats*. New York: Oxford University Press, 1964.

———. *James Joyce*. New York: Oxford University Press, 1959.

———. *Ulysses on the Liffey*. New York: Oxford University Press, 1972.

Fisch, Max Harold, and Bergin, Thomas Goddard. "Introduction" to the *Autobiography of Giambattista Vico*. Ithaca, N.Y.: Great Seal Books, a Division of Cornell University Press, 1963.

Ford, George H. *Dickens and His Readers: Aspects of Novel-Criticism Since 1836*. New York: Norton, 1965.

Forster, John. *The Life of Charles Dickens*. 2 Vols. New Edition with Notes and an Index by A. J. Hoppé and Additional Author's Footnotes. London: Dent and New York: Dutton, Everyman's Library, 1969.

France, Anatole. *Crainquebille, Putois, et Riquet*. Paris: Calmann-Lévy, editeurs, n.d.

Gilbert, Stuart. *James Joyce's ULYSSES*. New York: Knopf, 1930.

Givens, Seon, ed. *James Joyce: Two Decades of Criticism*. 2 Vols. New York: The Vanguard Press, 1948. New Introduction, 1963.

Glasheen, Adaline. *A Second Census of FINNEGANS WAKE: An Index of the Characters and their Roles*. Revised and expanded from the *First Census* by Adaline Glasheen. Includes the Foreword to the *First Census* by Richard Ellmann. Evanston, Ill.: Northwestern University Press, 1963.

Gorman, Herbert. *James Joyce*. New York: Rinehart, 1939; rev. ed., 1948.

Selected Bibliography

Hanley, Miles L. *Word Index to James Joyce's ULYSSES*. Madison: University of Wisconsin Press, 1965.

Hart, Clive. *A Concordance to FINNEGANS WAKE*. Minneapolis: University of Minnesota Press, 1963; rpt., Corrected Edition, Mamaroneck, N.Y.: Paul P. Appel, 1974.

――――. *Structure and Motif in FINNEGANS WAKE*. Evanston, Ill.: Northwestern University Press, 1962.

Hayman, David. *Joyce et Mallarmé: Stylistique de la Suggestion*. 2 Vols. Paris: Lettres Modernes, 1956.

Johnson, Edgar. *Charles Dickens: His Tragedy and Triumph*. 2 Vols. New York: Simon and Schuster, 1952.

Joyce, James, *The Critical Writings of James Joyce*. Edited by Ellsworth Mason and Richard Ellmann. New York: The Viking Press, 1959.

――――. "Daniel Defoe." Edited from Italian MSS. and translated by Joseph Prescott. *Buffalo Studies* (A Continuation of the "University of Buffalo Studies"), pub. by the State Univ. of New York at Buffalo. Vol. I, No. 1, Dec., 1964.

――――. *Dubliners: Text, Criticism, and Notes*. Edited by Robert Scholes and A. Walton Litz. New York: The Viking Press, 1969.

――――. *Finnegans Wake*. New York: The Viking Press, 1939.

――――. *Giacomo Joyce*. With an Introduction and Notes by Richard Ellmann. New York: The Viking Press, 1968.

――――. *Letters of James Joyce*. Edited by Stuart Gilbert. New York: The Viking Press, 1957; re-issued with corrections, 1966.

――――. *Letters of James Joyce*. Edited by Richard Ellmann. 2 Vols. New York: The Viking Press, 1966.

――――. *A Portrait of the Artist as a Young Man: Text, Criticism, and Notes*. Edited by Chester G. Anderson. New York: The Viking Press, 1968.

――――. *Selected Letters*. Edited by Richard Ellmann. New York: The Viking Press, 1975.

――――. *Stephen Hero*. Edited from the MSS. in the Harvard College Library by Theodore Spencer. A new edition, incorporating the additional MSS. pages in the Yale University Library and the Cornell University Library, edited by John J. Slocum and Herbert Cahoon. Norfolk, Conn.: New Directions, 1963.

――――. *Ulysses*. New York: Random House, 1961.

Joyce, Stanislaus. *The Complete Dublin Diary of Stanislaus Joyce.* Edited by George Harris Healey. Ithaca, N.Y.: Cornell University Press, 1962.

———. *My Brother's Keeper: James Joyce's Early Years.* Edited with an introduction and notes by Richard Ellmann. Preface by T. S. Eliot. New York: The Viking Press, 1958.

The Joyce Book. London: The Sylvan Press and H. Milford, Oxford University Press, 1933. "Epilogue" by Arthur Symons.

Kain, Richard M., ed. "An Interview with Carola Giedion-Welcker and Maria Jolas." *James Joyce Quarterly.* Vol. II, No. 2, Winter, 1974.

Kenner, Hugh. *Dublin's Joyce.* Bloomington, Ind.: University of Indiana Press, 1956.

Klein, A. M. "Shout in the Street: An Analysis of the Second Chapter of Joyce's ULYSSES." *New Directions,* 13. Norfolk: New Directions Books, 1951.

Levin, Harry. *James Joyce: A Critical Introduction.* Norfolk, Conn.: New Directions, 1941. Revised and augmented, 1960.

Maeterlinck, Maurice. *Pelléas and Mélisande.* Translated by Erving Winslow with an Introduction by Montrose J. Moses. New York: Thomas Y. Crowell, 1904 and 1908.

McIntyre, J. Lewis. *Giordano Bruno.* London and New York: Macmillan, 1903.

Nordau, Max. *Degeneration.* New York: D. Appleton, 1895.

O Hehir, Brendan. *A Gaelic Lexicon for Finnegans Wake and Glossary for Joyce's Other Works.* Berkeley and Los Angeles: University of California Press, 1967.

Paulson, Ronald. *Hogarth: His Life, Art, and Times.* Abridged by Anne Wilde. New Haven and London: Yale University Press, 1974.

Pinguentini, Gianni. *James Joyce in Italia.* Verona: Linotipia Veronese di Ghidini e Fiorini, 1963.

Pope-Hennessey, Una. *Charles Dickens.* New York: Howell, Soskin, 1946.

Power, Arthur. *Conversations with James Joyce.* Edited by Clive Hart. London: Willington, Ltd., 1974.

Praga, Marco. *La Crisi.* Milano: Fratelli Treves, Editori, 1904.

Reynolds, Mary T. "Joyce's Villanelle and D'Annunzio's Sonnet

Selected Bibliography

Sequence." *Journal of Modern Literature.* Vol. 5, No. 1, Feb., 1976, pp. 19–45.

Symons, Arthur. "Gabriele D'Annunzio" in *Studies in Prose and Verse.* London: Dent and New York: Dutton, 1904.

———. "Introduction" to Gabriele D'Annunzio's *The Child of Pleasure.* Translated by Georgina Harding with verses translated and an Introduction by Arthur Symons. Boston: The St. Botolph Society, 1898.

———. *The Symbolist Movement in Literature.* With an Introduction by Richard Ellmann. New York: E. P. Dutton and Co., Inc., 1958.

Scholes, Robert. *The Cornell Joyce Collection.* Ithaca: Cornell University Press, 1961.

———, and Kain, Richard M. *The Workshop of Daedalus: James Joyce and the Raw Materials for A PORTRAIT OF THE ARTIST AS A YOUNG MAN.* Evanston, Ill.: Northwestern University Press, 1965.

Smith, G. Barnett. *The Life of the Right Honourable William Ewart Gladstone.* London, Paris, New York: Cassell, Petter, Galpin and Co., 1881.

Spielberg, Peter. *James Joyce's Manuscripts and Letters at the University of Buffalo: A Catalogue.* Compiled and with an Introduction by Peter Spielberg. Buffalo: University of Buffalo Publication, 1963.

Tagliacozzo, Giorgio, and White, Hayden V., eds. *Giambattista Vico: An International Symposium.* Baltimore: The Johns Hopkins University Press, 1969.

———, and Verene, Donald Phillip, eds. *Giambattista Vico's Science of Humanity.* Baltimore and London: The Johns Hopkins University Press, 1976.

Thornton, Weldon. *Allusions in ULYSSES: An Annotated List.* Chapel Hill, N.C.: The University of North Carolina Press, 1968.

Turgenev, Ivan. *Smoke.* Translated by Natalie Duddington and introduced by Nikolay Andreyev. London: Dent and New York: Dutton, Everyman's Library, 1970.

Vico, Giambattista. *The Autobiography of Giambattista Vico.* Translation and Introduction by Max Harold Fisch and Thomas Goddard Bergin. Ithaca, N.Y.: Great Seal Books, A Division of Cornell University Press, 1963.

————. *The New Science.* Revised translation of the Third Edition (1744) by Thomas Goddard Bergin and Max Harold Fisch. Ithaca, N.Y.: Cornell University Press, 1968.

Yeats, William Butler. *The Celtic Twilight.* London: A. H. Bullen, 1902.

————. *Essays and Introductions.* New York: Macmillan, 1961.

————. Preface to *The Unicorn from the Stars and Other Plays.* New York: The Macmillan Co., 1908.

PROFESSOR LOUIS BERRONE received his B.A. and M.A. degrees from Trinity College, Hartford, and his Ph.D. from Fordham University. He studied at the Yale School of Drama, and has written plays, poetry, and opera libretti. A member of the James Joyce Society of New York City, The James Joyce Foundation, Ltd., the Dickens Fellowship, The Dickens Society of America, and the Modern Language Association, he has had articles published in several journals and reviews, including *The Dickensian* and *The Journal of Modern Literature*. He has lectured extensively in this country and abroad. He now lives in Woodbridge, Connecticut and is a professor of English at Fairfield University.